Celebrations

A SCRAPBOOK of IMAGINATIVE IDEAS for GALA DAYS

CONTENTS

6 · INTRODUCTION

10 · CHRISTENING

18 · ST VALENTINE'S DAY DINNER

24 · EASTER PARADE

36 · MAY DAY PICNIC

44 · WELL DRESSING

50 · WEDDING DAY

62 · PIRATE PARTY

74 · PRE-THEATRE PICNIC

78 · GARDEN FÊTE

94 · CARNIVAL

100 · BEACH PARTY

110 · HARVEST SUPPER

120 · GOLDEN WEDDING

130 · HOUSEWARMING

134 · CHRISTMAS

146 · NEW YEAR'S EVE MASKED BALL

158 · INDEX

INTRODUCTION

I have placed the hauntingly beautiful area of the far west of Cornwall at the heart of my book. It is my own home county, and thus illustrates the theme of the book – a very personal approach to setting the scene for celebrating a year's special events from St Valentine's Day to Christmas, and encompassing, among others, a christening, a wedding, a harvest supper and a country fête. I do, however, encourage people to think how they might individually reset these scenes in their own locality. The treatment for each occasion can be very simply translated; it just needs to be given a fresh emphasis. Inspired amateurism is what is needed, a few rough ends to awaken the spirit of these ancient festivals, so that they regain their own particular uniqueness.

To call a halt to these empty routines, we must be prepared to put more of ourselves into our plans and preparations for special occasions. We can then return to the well-placed priorities of our forebears before their practices are lost and become just memories. In their day, the calendar of festivals was truly star-studded, and people's lives throughout the year were punctuated by rich and exciting high days and holidays, which were eagerly awaited and savoured, season by season. In the same way, I have grouped the events in this book under the headings of spring, summer, autumn and winter, as the seasons play a dominant role in the location and atmosphere of any celebration.

SPRING

The warmth of a Cornish spring brings early flowers to the small pockets of fields along the peninsula's southern coastline. Whilst its famous gardens suddenly splash into life with huge treefuls of exotic blooms – camellias, magnolias and later azaleas – seas of sharp fresh green ferns are unfurling and expanding in great variety, the perfect camouflage for hiding painted eggs. Cliffs are suddenly studded with cushions of millefleur, wind-cropped alpine gems. The region's pagan past is to be found in the May Day celebrations centred around particular fields, spring wells and market towns. Parish feast days still lead to picnic expeditions and singing and dancing through the streets.

SUMMER

Decked out for its summer season, Cornwall is all blond and blues as the sand and sea dominate. This is how she is best known. The central backbone of the country is vacated as everyone radiates out to its crusty edges to picnic among its rocks and pools, returning from the beach with skin lightly scorched by that exhilarating mixture of sun and wind. This is also carnival time, which sees gaudily festooned trailers progress through steep and crowded streets to the water's edge. In sub-tropical gardens afternoon fêtes offer summer's abundance, set out on stalls canopied for shade or sudden showers. At the spectacular open-air theatre on the cliff the waiting evening audience watch the white *Scillonion* cruise by returning with its passengers from the Isles of Scilly. Beacon fires are lit to mark the summer solstice, whilst a gentler fire is used for cooking the catch in the softening light at a beach party.

AUTUMN

Autumns are short in Cornwall when the first gales sweep in with salt-laden winds. The leaves on the stunted trees are quick to shrivel and fall. They barely have time to change colour. The cliffs at this time are spectacular, aglow with the coppery bracken which sweeps across contours only halted in its progress on meeting the jagged, ever-yellow bushes of gorse. The blue brilliance of the sea fades to a heartbreaking softer grey-green and its surface roughens, working up to its winter turmoil. The year-long toil of the farmers, who pace out their activities oblivious to all but the weather, now comes into focus. Every step and ledge of the village churches is crammed with the fruits of their labour, brought in for the services of thanksgiving. The pubs hold boisterous auctions selling off the produce at exaggerated prices for charity. There is now a lull and a time for pleasure before the ploughing starts the yearly cycle again.

WINTER

In winter Cornwall braces itself for the second onslaught of the year after the tourist invasion of summer. The paradox of these winters is such that one week you are summoning all your mettle to live through a hell-raising storm, and the next, strolling on a stretch of sunlit sand. It is said that Cornish winters are mild, and that is so, in terms of temperature. However, with nothing between us and the Americas, the wind can reach horrendous strengths by the time it gets to our ragged peninsula. When the wind has howled one day too long, the calendar of yearly events conveniently provides distractions. The company of other people is sought and the Christmas period, with all its attendant activities of preparation and celebration, is welcomed.

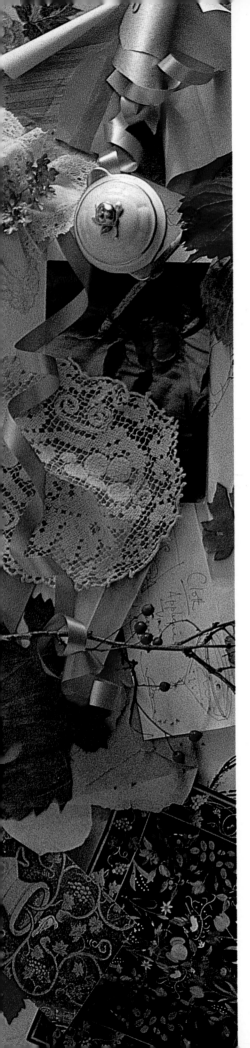

INSPIRATION

The *raison d'être* of this book is the creation of stunning effects through the simplest materials used with the greatest possible ingenuity. To trigger off the preparations for each event, I have used collage sheets, fragments of tentative thinking that are assembled together for the purpose of inspiration.

I have suggested making these collages as an aid to clear planning. At this stage, when intuitive ideas are passing through one's head, it is essential to record them freshly, as the first are most frequently the best, however seemingly ambitious and absurd at the time. It is easy then to weed them out at a later stage. They form a basic starting point to the important question of defining the style of an event. In the past I have instinctively done this in a very unstructured way; however, for the purpose of this book, this stage has been clearly thought through and pinned down.

I have found these 'tachiste' sheets really useful, particularly at those moments of doubt which sweep over you when under pressure to make a decision. I shall now undoubtedly use them as a device for the planning of any future family event.

Begin by assembling a cohesive pile of oddments, things that look pleasing together. Gather scraps of this and that, such as a strip of moiré ribbon, wine-coloured, that looks so elegant laid next to a piece of nubbly ashen lace on a dull-green sugar paper background. This sort of exercise will help develop nuances of ideas which build up to that necessary sense of drama to make your party both glamorous and highly personal.

COLOUR

An area where I have found my collage sheets of particular value is in defining the colours that are to dominate as a keynote to an event. Scraps of paper torn from magazines or household packets, the coloured lining of envelopes and paper bags all help with this definition. I have even retrieved tickets from the floor of a bus because they were a particular sort of green or pink. Ephemera as disparate as a pale grey dried-out leaf, a fragment of rosy chair covering or a bright plastic bag may express the exact nuance of colour you feel is right. Combining colours is such a subtle process. Think how seldom you find exactly the right combination on a range of paint cards selected by expert marketing advisers, and you can see how wonderfully personal and versatile the whole issue is.

MATERIALS

Choosing from the basic *natural materials* for my projects was both easy and a pleasure. There is something of an inbred ease about handling such substances. We worked with muslins, cottons and canvas, ropes and strings, also papers, cardboards and candles. Selecting from *natural elements* we have decorated with flowers, wild and cultivated, cut, potted and dried. We have used whole trees and bushes, branches, twigs, leaves and many kinds of cut wood. Feathers and eggs, seaweed and shells have also been gathered to further our creative cause.

As for *man-made materials*, I have called on the new magic of plastics and polythenes, also nylons in the form of textiles, cords, nets, ribbons and laces. In metals I have used ordinary tin cans, meshes and wires, and to transform and glamorize many of these surfaces we have coated and embellished with numerous paints and varnishes, variously enhancing them with matt, shiny and metallic finishes. Most of these marvellous materials require particular gluing agents so I have sprayed, gummed, smeared and brushed on a fair number of diverse adhesive solutions ranging from flour-and-water paste to sophisticated contact glue.

You will usually know from the outset, when planning an event, whether it is to be set indoors or out. This will affect the quality of the materials to be used: robust or fragile, precious or disposable. The materials, while being beautiful in their own right, must also be practical, as were the bright blue polythene rubbish bags which we split up to line the rough orange-box trays for picnic suppers at the outdoor cliff-side theatre. Another example of raising the status of a lowly, utilitarian material was when cheap feather dusters were plucked of their turquoise feathers to adorn the masks we made for the New Year's Ball.

Among other materials that can be utilized are bundles of long-hoarded strips of ribbons and cards of lace, at last justified and coming into their own. They may have precisely the right hue and texture to tie a parcel or a bunch of flowers. The satisfaction that comes from putting time and substance together with a sense of 'rightness' is considerable.

It is the same with cloth. Take that yellow Indian bedspread bought purely because something about the intensity of its pattern momentarily appealed, not because you needed it to cover a bed. This can be pulled out at last to envelop a table and decorated with a huge green glass bowl filled with alstromeria, which will complement those garish green plates from Aunty Flo. At last your impromptu purchase stands exonerated. Add some cheap and colourful Polish wine-glasses and plenty of those yellowing candles from the back of a drawer, and this will not feel 'everyday', but rather a suitably colourful and bizarre supper table to welcome the sudden appearance of a globe-trotting offspring. Home is not so dreary after all. As we are all chased by life, the importance of some extra gestures marks out and compliments the recipient.

STENCILLING

Many decorative techniques have been used to transform plain surfaces. However, as stencilling is now like a native language to me, I have called upon this immensely versatile craft almost subconsciously. A large number of the decorative illusions created throughout the pages of this book are brought to fruition by its deceptively simple use. Whether it is golden foliage mapped out across some richly coloured felt or a skull-and-cross-bones stamped on to a sack, the basic process is the same. A sheet of card has a design cut out of it and when the card is placed over a surface, paint is applied through the cut-away holes. A primitively simple method for printing repeated patterns. All manner of styles have been defined by this crude method from the most naive to the ambitiously grand.

It was with some sense of fun that we dallied with half-remembered childlike occupations such as printing with potato cuts, gumming up paper-chains and modelling with dough.

FOOD

I have involved myself in offering only a few visual suggestions on the subject of food, for this is not a cookery book. Dishes are there as pointers to possible directions to take. At many events a decorated cake stands as a symbolic centrepiece. The making of such a cake is often a warmingly primitive activity, that fortunately we still practise; we must not let it slip away from our hands to become commercially vacuous. Put together with a variety of skills, it is not just the thought that counts, but every choice that goes into the making of the cake, right down to its trimming.

It is not only cakes that have a symbolic connotation in matters of food; so, too, do the harvests of land and sea. The apple has been marked out as a symbol of fertility, and since biblical time the fish and the loaf of bread have been symbols of plenty. In Cornwall Star Gazey Pie, with fishes' heads and tails poking out from its golden crust, is not best known for its culinary heights but as a reminder of a fisherman, one Tom Bawcock, who braved the roaring ocean to bring back fish and saved his community from starving one Christmas.

Often the preparation of the food as well as the cooking itself is an enjoyable part of an event, for example, the stirring of the Christmas pudding when the silver coins are dropped into the dark sticky mixture and wishes are made.

While not adhering slavishly to colour schemes in the choice and preparation of dishes, there is no doubt that a delicately sympathetic colour connection is needed and can be fun. The point is that the food need not be perfect, but the choices should be very personal and respect the fads and favourites of your family This avoids the dreary repetition of so-called 'suitable' dishes.

Specially made tablecloths, napkins and cushions also add to the excitement of a meal, and you can pick out your chosen colour schemes with these furnishings. Decorated for the day, they remain as evocative reminders of your feast.

Spring

CHRISTENING

A CHRISTENING CEREMONY REPRESENTS THE PUREST OF CELEBRATIONS, A
PRIMAL WELCOMING OF A NEW LIFE. WHAT COULD BE MORE JOYOUS?
CANDLES ARE LIT AND HELD BY GODPARENTS AS THEY MAKE PROMISES OF
PROTECTION AND GUIDANCE. THE FLOWERS WREATHING THE FONT AND
COLUMN ARE BROUGHT TO THE CHURCH IN THE EARLY MORNING.

*Blue flowers and acid greenery form a generous wreath around the vast lead-
lined bowl of this ancient font (left). Christening presents are unwrapped on a
side table: a christening mug, a prayer book and a pincushion (above).*

Inspiration

Mother-of-pearl is the inspiration behind the fragile colouring chosen for the christening, a gentle background that will not overwhelm the small baby around whom it is all centred. Silvery hints of green-blue and pink are merely suggested. The party will be held in a room which enjoys the classic colour combination of eau-de-nil and gold, which, together with my all-time favourite ivory, will stop it from becoming too sweet.

Spring is the perfect time for this occasion with all its symbolic connotations of new life, and the wonderful profusion of spring flowers can naturally enhance our celebration. The gentle colouring of herbs is planned for the font in the country church and masses of mostly white blooms for the house. They will look so fresh against the pale green walls.

There is a plan to plant a Japanese cherry tree in the garden after the service to mark the day. A tin name tag has been hammered out with the baby's name to label it separately. Over the years, she can go to it and measure herself up against the growth of the tree. This glinting tag made of tin shares a dotted metallic quality with the cushion's pattern of steel pinheads.

Dressmaker's interfacing has a strange and interestingly unfamiliar feel; used out of context and snipped into decorative bows, it is particularly pretty with some silky ribbons in pastel shades. An antique element is introduced in the working of a sampler, an idea to revive and present, suitably inscribed with the personal details of the baby. The tiny pair of embroidered Chinese slippers is given for hanging decoratively from a ribbon on the nursery wall, rather than for any practical use.

To bring a child to church to be named and accepted into a community is a time-honoured custom. The fourteenth-century font in the church at Sancreed stands as a powerful reminder of just how ancient this practice is. Locally, the baptismal waters are taken from particular springs that have, over the centuries, been invested with the title of Holy Wells. These holy wells often have small, medieval chapels built beside them, known as baptistries.

We have surrounded the font with flowers and herbs from the garden: forget-me-nots and yellow marjoram, rosemary and the grey-leaved curry plant, rue and acid yellow fennel flowers. At the base sinuous sprays of ivy follow the contours of

Presents are wrapped with stencilled ribbons, cut away Vilene bows and tiny moulded doves (far right). A commemorative pincushion, with its message marked out in pins, has additional trimmings of tassels and pearls (right).

A pristine antique christening robe, constructed with infinite delicacy from finely embroidered lawn, lies across an oak cradle with godparents' presents of silver and a mother-of-pearl scoop for the baptismal water (above).

the hewn granite, just as it clings to the walls outside the church, and clematis is wound around the top of a stone column to fall away loosely and hang above the font. Four crowned angels of granite guard the font from which the water is poured gently on to the child's forehead as part of this custom of anointing.

The christening robe of the finest white cotton lawn is passed down through generations. The quality of its embroidery is the subject of much admiration with sighs of disbelief at the finesse of the stitching.

The tradition of godparents giving gifts of

silver continues today with christening mugs, rattles and, to little girls, tiny necklaces. They seem somehow medieval, like the gift of life's first chattels. A small pottery drinking mug, specially made with the new name inscribed on it, would seem more practical for today. However, the charm of these classical gifts is undeniable; extravagant, precious and personal, they are nostalgically treasured throughout life.

It is a Swedish custom to have a child's name on the wall above the bed where they sleep, and as a variation on the idea of painting straight on to the fabric of a wall, I have painted a panel with the name. I choose to paint this particular panel because it was already painted with a beautiful dusky pink across its surface. On to its receptive matt texture I painted a creamy heart with the name Tamzin and her date of birth. Then I added some freely painted boughs of deep green leaves with birds lodging in them. This can eventually go with her wherever she pleases, even eventually forming a bedhead for her grown-up bed.

COMMEMORATIVE PINCUSHION

Blue and pink are colours that were frequently counterbalanced on Edwardian commemorative pincushions. Highly decorated, colourful beads and sequins were worked in as part of the pinwork. Pincushions such as these were given as presents to commemorate special days ranging from the start of a new year to the start of a new life. Appropriate messages were spelt out in pinheads, such as 'Welcome little stranger'.

Quite simply I make a small square cushion out of pale green suede cloth and densely stuff it with kapok. The close-cropped pile makes an ideal background texture for the pins. I work freehand, making up the patterns to fill in around the words as I go along. However, it might be easier to map out the pattern on a piece of tracing paper the same size. After laying this over the cushion and securing it, the pattern can be worked through the paper guide which can afterwards be torn away. I use some pins with pearl heads saved from the packaging of a new shirt to highlight the design. Braids and tassels are glued into position and this unusual gift is ready to be wrapped.

MAKING PRESENT WRAPPING
IF YOU MAKE YOUR OWN SPECIAL
WRAPPING FOR PRESENTS, YOU CAN
BE SURE THEY WILL BE VERY APT AND
PERSONAL AND NOT IN THE LEAST
BIT AT ODDS WITH THE GIFT INSIDE. I
HAVE CHOSEN PALE SOFT COLOURS
AS BEFITS A GIFT TO THE VERY
YOUNG. BROAD WHITE PETERSHAM
RIBBON HAS BEEN STENCILLED WITH
PAIRS OF BLUE BIRDS, THEIR BEAKS
FULL OF LEAVES FOR THEIR NESTS.
MORE BIRDS, MADE OF WHITE
PLASTIC FOR CAKE-TOPS, ARE FIXED
INTO THE CENTRE OF FRILLY BOWS

CUT WITH SERRATED EDGES FROM
DRESSMAKER'S INTERFACING. THEY
LOOK AS IF THEY MIGHT FLY AWAY
AT ANY MOMENT. A SMALL BIBLE IS
WRAPPED IN SOME OF OUR GOLD
CLOTH, TIED WITH SPARKLING BLUE
AND PINK RICRAC AND FINISHED OFF
WITH TWO WHITE BIRDS.

The powdery-green painted panelling of this airy room makes a delicate backdrop for the christening party. Furnished over many centuries, it is my husband's old family house. The fabric of the room has some finely honed detailing in the form of the panelling, moulding and glazing, as seen on the tall Gothic doors of the china cabinets. Great armfuls of Queen Anne's lace (common cow parsley) are held in glass vases and set behind a pair of Dresden shepherdesses. This particular room, with all its accoutrements, is beautiful, but it is mainly the richness of the cloth and the festive look of all the flowers that set the mood and that would enliven most rooms. A delightful heady scent of creamy stocks, lilies-of-the-valley and white narcissi pervades the room.

Tea is laid out on the side table and everything is ready for the christening party to return from church. An old-fashioned urn will ease the task of pouring the tea; a turn of the tap will fill the pretty gold-rimmed cups. For this is an occasion to reach deep into the china cupboard and bring out the best tea service. It has been waiting there for such an event, for such happenings are few and far between these days. Tea sipped from a cup with a fine thin rim is an extra pleasure to enjoy on this leisurely afternoon. Small triangular sandwiches with cucumber, salmon and anchovy fillings, snippets of celery with cream cheese and capers, melba toast and fish pâté offer a variety of savoury tastes before the sweetness of meringues and sugary cake.

Traditionally the top tier of the wedding cake was preserved for the christening of the first child. Much is made of the presentation of the cake, adorned with fresh flowers and white- and silver-coated sugared almonds. The original fluted vase is filled with fresh flowers and a sentimental little white lace cradle has been added to the top.

The lively texture of the gold tablecloth is very easily achieved. Cambric is measured to cover the table to the ground. Cut in two strips and joined together down the middle, it makes a square which allows 8 cm (3 in) all round for a nice deep hem. After folding the sewn cambric into quarters, a length of curtain netting is laid diagonally across to cover the two folded sides. Its dec-

orative border runs across the middle, forming a new 'edge' for this illusory lacy cloth.

Spray this quarter of the cambric generously with gold paint, then repeat the process on the three other quarters of the cloth in turn, pausing for a little drying time between each. The aim is not to get a perfect resist print from the lace but a slightly hesitant, misty patterning.

Open it all out and you will find a new lacy

The cake is ringed with lacy white flowers. Tucked in between are tiny silver comfit dishes of sugared almonds. A white lace cradle is made on a wire frame for the top of the cake; trimmings are made with dots of white icing (left). The christening tea is laid out on a lavish yet home-made gold cloth.

cloth superimposed over the larger gold one. Placed over the table, this sweepingly stagy accessory is just the sort of look that is needed to distinguish and uplift what could be an ordinary family gathering. If there is no time to make a tablecloth like this, you can always buy a cheap plain tablecloth, spray it with the same gold paint, and when it has dried, place another of real lace over it. Not as subtle, but very pretty.

Ties holding back the long parchment curtains have been specially made as part of the dressing-up for the party. A cheap lace cloth with a coarser design has been sprayed through this time with its unpatterned scalloped edge cut crisply away. Looped loosely around the curtains, the tie-backs look lavish and effortless. They prove, yet again, that a look of luxury can easily be obtained with a little ingenuity.

ST VALENTINE'S DAY DINNER

IT IS COMMON KNOWLEDGE THAT A TRULY ROMANTIC GESTURE IS A RARE
THING THESE DAYS. MEN HAVE FORGOTTEN HOW TO MAKE THEM AND WOMEN
DON'T KNOW HOW TO RECEIVE THEM. TO TAKE TIME AND TROUBLE SECRETLY
TO MAKE AN OCCASION MEMORABLE FOR SOMEONE IS VERY FLATTERING. A
PERSON CAN FLOWER AS THE FOCUS OF SUCH ATTENTION AND HEARTS CAN
BE WON. ST VALENTINE'S DAY IS THE EVENING OF ALL THE YEAR THAT
IS MOST CONDUCIVE TO A ROMANTIC SUPPER.

A table set for a private supper for two overlooking the green water of the inner harbour (left).
By the window, a diamond ring is tied by a piece of lace and some pale ribbon to a Valentine
card, and a delicate pear sorbet topped with crystallized violets is served (above).

Inspiration

To create a romantic setting for St Valentine's Day, I have visualized a table by a window, intimately set with two chairs; a cloth sweeps to the floor where a bucket of champagne has been set down. The table is full of luxurious clutter, cards, flowers, chocolates, wine and ribbons. I plan to carry this through in a palette of fragile, watery colouring, astringent and fresh, assiduously avoiding anything too syrupy. Silvery greys to contrast with deeper tones of green and purple, mere dashes of mauve with a subdued pink being kept to an absolute minimum. White, beige and silver represent the cooler neutral colours.

This primarily sentimental occasion with trappings of flowers and gifts provides an opportunity to express feelings that are too often neglected. The Victorians made much of it, producing delicately decorated and embossed cards inscribed with sentiments that are too flowery for us today.

They also made some beautiful jewellery to commemorate these unions of the heart. Fine lockets and brooches will open out and reveal sepia images of particular loved ones. It is poignant to look at them now and think of the strength of feeling with which they were offered and accepted.

Jewellery is still occasionally given by sweethearts on St Valentine's Day. Rings are favoured, but lockets have fallen from fashion except perhaps as gifts to children. It is sad, for I think they are a beautiful concept, particularly if they are as fine as the one made of ebony, inlaid with mother-of-pearl, illustrated here, which I was given and treasure. There are many old lockets about still, handed down or found in antique shops.

When threaded up with ribbon they could at least be worn each Valentine's Day to ensure that the romantic traditions of wearing lockets are not lost to us.

A Valentine Card

SLIPPING A SMALL RING-CASE OUT
OF A JACKET POCKET AT A
PARTICULARLY APPROPRIATE
MOMENT IS THE USUAL FORM. BUT
WHAT IF A DIAMOND SHOULD GLINT
AND CATCH THE EYE AS IT DANGLES
FROM A RIBBON ON A VALENTINE
CARD? THE IMMEDIATE,
SUBCONSCIOUSLY REGISTERED
IMPLICATION WOULD MAKE IT A
THRILLINGLY ROMANTIC GESTURE.
OUR CARD, LIKE A SMALL
VICTORIAN POSY WITH A HEART IN
THE CENTRE, IS MADE UP OF A PIECE
OF PINK ANTIQUE BROCADE RIBBON,
FLOWER HEADS AND PAPER DOILY
LACE. THESE ARE ARRANGED AND
STUCK DOWN ON A DISC OF
CARDBOARD APPROXIMATELY 15 CM
(6 IN) IN DIAMETER WITH FABRIC OR
PAPER GLUE. THE RUCHED-UP PICOT
RIBBON AROUND THE CLOTH HEART
ENDS IN LONG TIES. THE RING IS
SECURED WITH A KNOT OF WHITE
LACE. PROPPED NONCHALANTLY
AGAINST THE WINDOW, IT IS ASKING
TO BE NOTICED.

St Valentine is the patron saint of lovers and it was suggested by Chaucer that birds paired on that day. The main activity that 14th February brings about these days is the secret sending of all manner of cards, from the frankly sentimental to the mildly abusive. The date provides an opportunity to declare a secret passion or tease a colleague, while still remaining under-cover. However, the most popular and welcome expression of love is today, as it ever was, a gift of flowers. From the simplest garden flowers to hothouse blooms, 'it is said with flowers'. I would myself always prefer to receive simple, undressed flowers, such as a box full of anemones, than contorted cellophane-wrapped confections of more expensive blooms.

On a part of low-lying Cornish coastline that faces due south are small pockets of fields that are particularly sheltered, frost-free and fertile. Stretching sporadically from Mousehole to St Loy, these are the violet fields that provided the favourite flowers for Victorian England. Bunched in the fields as they were picked, each posy was enveloped in a deeply dark green ivy leaf, the perfect foil. Taken straight to London from Brunel's elegant railway station at Penzance, they had to be in Covent Garden in time for the early market.

Today our lovers' choice is still violets, dozens of tight little bunches of powerful purple flowers, exuding their heavy scent into the evening air. We crowd them into a deep silver lustre bowl to drink deeply before placing them on the table.

THE SETTING

In an upper room of the hotel, curtains are pulled back and a round table is pushed up to the window. Two chairs are drawn up to the table to enjoy the fine harbour view before the light fades. A white lace cloth is spread and the table laid with the prettiest china, silver and glass. Beige lacy mats with designs of small flying birds are placed under the plates.

An extravagant supper of crayfish salad and fruit sorbet is planned with celebratory champagne. Minute cut glasses are laid for the exquisite Poire William followed by a small cup of Java coffee.

An old heart-shaped chocolate box is completely revamped and filled with specially handmade chocolates and truffles. It is first covered in lace-printed paper, then elaborately trimmed with ricrac braid and cords which have been separately sprayed with different densities of gold paint.

I find the intricately cut and embossed patterns of the much-scorned paper doily a great asset when wanting to create rich effects. To use on the chocolate box I carefully cut away some individual flower shapes and also some shell-like edging. Sprayed with gold they are transformed, as if by magic, into fragments of ancient gold embroidery. The flowers are fixed in clusters with beady centres and real dried leaves at the top of the box, and the shelling backs up the elaborate cording stuck around the rim.

When the paints and glue are thoroughly dry the box can be packed with cream and brown chocolates in little gold-fluted cases. They would not now look out of place in the window of a smart French Chocolate Shop. The scene is now set for the actors to appear and play their version of a memorable evening.

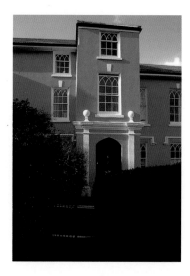

The old quayside house that is now the Abbey Hotel was built in 1660, its pretty Gothic windows being added later in Victorian times. They look out loftily over the inner harbour of Penzance and beyond it to St Michael's Mount and the ocean. This is the perfect place for our private supper party (above).

To keep the champagne cool we have had fun with a new galvanized bucket. I have always thought their misty pewter surface attractive, and stencilled round their ribbed exterior they look quite transformed. On the first band we cheat and use a strip of lace to give it some expensive-looking gold etched scallops. The next is simply a row of hearts, applied with pink paints spattered with gold, while on the broadest band we depict an elaborate pair of floating cupids (left).

EASTER PARADE

A CHILDREN'S PARTY AT EASTERTIME CAN BE A JOYFUL OCCASION. RELEASED OUT OF DOORS AT LAST, AFTER BEING COOPED UP FOR ALL THOSE LONG, DARK DAYS, THEY REVEL IN THE NEW FREEDOM. FOLLOWING A TRAIL THROUGH THE WOODS, THEY HUNT FOR EGGS AMONG THE FRESH FOLIAGE, NEW GROWTH INDUCED BY THE RETURNING WARMTH. THIS GAME OF HIDE 'N' SEEK HAS A TIMELESS APPEAL, WHETHER IN ENCLOSED GARDENS OR OPEN COUNTRYSIDE.

Children search for eggs which are artfully concealed in picturesque groups among the undergrowth (left). Small basketfuls of spotted painted eggs nestling in shredded paper and a discarded paper bonnet on a specially-painted chair (above).

Inspiration

There is a pale brightness about the bits and pieces I have collected together to express the mood of the Easter celebrations, which being held outdoors are immediately relaxing and exciting. Colours are predominantly yellows, ranging from strong daffodil gold to watery primrose, but also include a deep sugary pink and a false sharp pistachio green. I have also added a lovely hyacinth blue. The Neapolitan colours of the printed tissues that individually wrap those delicious almond Amaretti biscuits precisely convey the visual and textural qualities I envisage: pastel colours like pale papery spring flowers.

Spots always have a way of looking fresh and appealing, and the spotted papers and ribbons I use for small parcels, cake frills and bonnet trimmings all have a fragile, pretty look. Easter bonnets are concocted from paper fripperies, odds and ends associated with the confectionery trade. Little fluted sweet cases, jelly cups, doilies and paper bakery ribbons are all cut, glued and coaxed into flowery trimmings.

Pictures of softly painted, roughly made wooden buildings are to inspire the construction of some fanciful animal enclosures to house rabbits and chicks – party diversions.

Sheets of tissue paper with pinked edges are sprayed with lime and pink spots and used as pretty wrapping paper. A fresh leafy salad has the added appeal of primroses as a garnish. Marzipan biscuits are stamped out in the shape of animals, birds and fishes (above). The tea party set in a sheltered corner of the garden is decorated with the fuchsia-pink chicks' pavilion and white rabbits made from plaster-of-Paris (below).

EASTER TEA

We carried the long kitchen table down to a low lawn, enclosed and sheltered by deep granite 'hedging'. These high banks are smothered with those early daisies, whose leaves turn a beautiful silver grey as summer approaches.

The table is spread with a generous counter-pane which has been carefully stencilled with scattered tufts of flowers. They are rather like those on the gown of the goddess of spring from the Botticelli painting, Primavera. A large white sheet could be given just the same treatment. Folding the cloth lengthwise, I have stencilled the images to face inwards from the hem so that when the cloth is laid over the table, the flowers are the right way up. The leaves are coloured first in sharp sap green turning into a mid-green. Next some gently gradated colours for the flower heads in golden yellow and deep campion pink are applied, masking them clear of the green with a strip of hand-held card.

All dressed up in fancy bonnets, it is time to sit up to the tea. The party food comes to the table on a mixture of leafy plates with pink-handled tea knives. The food is also leafy: salads, celery sticks, cress-and-egg sandwiches cut in small triangles of brown with white bread. A long leaf plate in a lovely shade of lavender blue has a pink creamy rabbit flopped from its mould on to it. A row of little coloured iced gem biscuits form a daisy chain around its base.

THE SIMNEL CAKE

The simnel cake's association with Eastertime dates back to at least the sixteenth century. The word 'simnel' refers to the white flour; the finest was always used for the baking. Some centuries later, it became the custom for young daughters, working away from home in service to some grand household, to make these cakes. They were then allowed to carry them back to their mothers as gifts for Mothering Sunday. The top of the cake is normally smothered in marzipan, but I have reduced this amount. As well as deeply cut serrated edges, a large star shape has been cut out from the top centre of the cake. The points of the star have been furled back to reveal the glazed cake beneath. Twelve marzipan balls spaced out around this star traditionally represent the twelve apostles. These balls and the marzipan surface are scorch-marked by a hot branding iron, then dusted with white icing sugar. Sitting on a raised plate-stand, the simnel cake is collared in layers of spotted netting, one of the party themes. It makes a splendid perch for our wistful group of Easter ducklings.

CHICKS' PAVILION

A fanciful pavilion cobbled together from off-cuts of plywood, narrow lengths of wood and small-gauge chicken wire, is like a gaudy Indian temple. On its outer surface it is painted a bright pink, then daubed with blue spots; its inside shell is a delicate eau-de-nil. On its sturdy, shaped base it is set down along the centre of the tablecloth. To the children's great delight, baby chicks strut up and down its length, eating and drinking from their little troughs.

EASTER EGG HUNT

The eggs that are sought out at Easter have to be particularly special. Hunted and found in nooks and crannies, far afield and in unlikely spots, they form part of the mysteries of childhood. Our trail leads through a garden into a bluebell wood, past an old water well and eventually down to a cove where the mottled eggs lie camouflaged in a niche between the smooth granite rocks.

On the day of the party we set to, around a garden table, aprons donned to decorate the eggs. We have a large mixing bowl full of them, in differing hues and sizes. The children find much quiet messy pleasure in daubing the receptive texture of the eggs with poster paints. Sometimes they stick little round labels and stars all over them, then when the eggs have been painted, pull them off - a simple process of resist. For coloured spots and stars, they must paint the egg twice, once before the shapes are stuck on, then again afterwards. For a really smooth, matt texture, spray paint can be used as the colouring agent.

An envelope full of old foreign stamps, of no intrinsic value, offers an opportunity to indulge in some childish découpage. Gummed to overlap all over the surface of the eggs, they can be sealed with a varnish and left to dry on four little stilts (dressmaker's pins, stuck firmly into a piece of wood). Other eggs that will need careful varnishing have small pressed flowerheads assembled in pretty groups glued to their surface. Some more eggs are boiled with onion skins to a rich glowing bronze. They are then patterned all over with bronze and gold pens.

The children concentrate on decorating their eggs with stars, spots and other fantastical paint decorations (above).

Eggs that have been given a botanical look, covered with pressed flowerheads, lie easily among the new ferns whilst a rich cache of patterned eggs, suspended in the tangled strands of a tree, have a Russian look about them. The texture of granite rocks is echoed in the mottled, muted colouring of this trio of eggs. Eggs painted like china to match their cups sit on the ledge of an old well (right).

RABBIT HUTCH

The rabbit house is made up from three old tea-chests, which are placed closely together on their sides on the ground, the two outer chests with their openings facing to the front, while the middle one faces backwards. This back opening later forms the entrance to the hutch, once a simple flap of plywood has been hinged to the top and the frame to cover it. A simple fastening at the base stops the rabbits getting out.

Prior to fixing the three cubes together, interconnecting circles are cut from their inner sides, big and low enough for a rabbit to leap through. This is the stage when their interiors are given a smart wash of pink paint. The chests are now joined together with timbers running along their full length at the top and bottom, front and back. These are nailed into the side of each frame.

Next, the front of the middle chest has a decorative pattern pierced and cut through with a jigsaw for extra ventilation. The other fronts have wire meshing fixed over them by means of an arched frame, its shape sawn out from odd scraps of plywood. Eight stumpy legs made from a piece of 5 x 5 cm (2 x 2 in) timber are fixed on to keep the hutch off the ground. These are discreetly covered by an apron of some more cut and pierced plywood arches.

An even more fanciful façade, reminiscent of circus props, is cut and fixed to span the top of the hutch. When this construction is complete, its outer surface is painted with a coat of soft blue emulsion. This glamorous residence is now ready for occupation.

EASTER BONNETS

Of course, children love dressing up and, surprisingly, even the shyest is eager to be transformed into another character. Merely by donning some recognizable style borrowed from a favourite storybook, they feel transported into another world. A bonnet such as might have been worn by Little-Bo-Peep or Lucy Locket, or a hat like Georgie Porgie's or even the Mad March Hare's at the tea party in Alice in Wonderland – these all add tremendously to the excitement.

Bakers and confectioners know a thing or two about presentation and we find the decorative paraphernalia of their trade extremely suitable for our project. Doilies with their stamped-out lacy patterns are a gift and there are many uses for them. Laid flat on the coloured cardboard discs, they are sprayed over like a stencil in different colours. This covers the cardboard with a lace-like texture and colours the doily at the same time. The edge of the scalloped shape, left by the imprint of the doily on the disc, can be cut carefully around. Other bonnets can have the edge of the card pinked with shears or they can be cut with ordinary scissors into deeper zigzags. Folded into fans, cut sections of the doilies can be tucked in as foliage around some 'flowers' made of knotted ribbons.

Little paper cases, the kind used for serving *petits fours* at the end of a dinner party, make a marvellous base for flowers. They come in just the colours we want to use. A number of fresh green cases have small balls of scrunched-up pink tissue paper stuck into their centres. These have been sprayed lightly with gold paint to give them a look of faded rosebuds. Set inside a deep lacy frill of lighter green, they make a very pretty frame for a pretty young face. On the outer rim of a deeper poke bonnet small blue and pink petals, set in a similar manner, look just as charming.

To decorate another bonnet, a waxy moulded jelly cup, which already has a scalloped petal edge cut deeply into its pleated rim, is cut across into sections. These are glued to the middle of a large cardboard disc and stand away beautifully, forming the outer petals of a flamboyant flower. The centre of this flower is made of a spread-out

tassel of colourfully sprayed cartridge paper. This is finished off with a small button of blue paper, securing a tail of curled streamers.

Continuing the floral theme, strips of tissue paper are cut with a curving serpentine edge and loosely rolled and flattened to resemble the multicoloured heads of hydrangea flowers, tightly grouped in an arc. The vivid green brim of this bonnet is pulled in, to tie demurely under the chin with wide pink and green ribbons. The ribbon with its satin sheen is normally used to

add a touch of glamour to boxed-up bakery treats. This luxury look, which belies its cheapness, makes it an invaluable asset to our collection of trimmings. It looks particularly appealing when its surface is stencilled with some simple motif.

All the time we have at hand cans of paints in the designated party colours, ready to add a splash of extra richness to any surface. Spraying across some holes cut through a piece of card readily creates some stylish spots. Final bonnet trimmings include stencilled butterflies with folding wings at the top of a ribbon and tiny yellow chicks perched around an upper brim.

EASTER BONNETS
USING SCRAPS OF EVERY KIND OF PAPER IMAGINABLE, WE CONCOCT SOME DELIGHTFUL CONFECTIONS OF THROW-AWAY MILLINERY. WELL BEFORE EASTER WE COLLECT TOGETHER A CARDBOARD BOX FULL OF PRETTY PAPERS, WRAPPINGS, PACKING AND RIBBONS – BITS AND PIECES YOU WOULD NORMALLY DISCARD. SITTING AROUND A TABLE HEAPED WITH THIS BOOTY, WE BEGIN RECYCLING IT INTO HATS AND BONNETS. TRIMMED WITH FLOWERS, BUTTERFLIES AND RIBBONS MADE OF PAPER, WE AIM TO CONJURE UP 'THE SWEETEST BONNET IN THE EASTER PARADE'.

MAY DAY PICNIC

When the heart of a community was truly based around the rural calendar, the coming of May was set aside for treats and holidays. The young people gathered in particular fields and woods for sports, games and a special tea treat. The setting for this gathering is under a favourite apple tree in a sheltered corner where the sun dapples through on to the tea below. Cakes and tarts are laid out on a special cloth and surrounded with matching cushions.

*Ribbons made of pretty ginghams give a festive look to our orchard setting
(left). Freshly picked daisies crown the young May queens and home-made
lemonade is served (above).*

Inspiration

The emergence of the new growth, pale shoots and leaf buds of earliest summer, seems like a miracle after the long grey winter months. The unleashing of the freshest green foliage and the purest of pale, unfurling spring flowers is what May Day celebrations are all about. Since time immemorial it has presented a most delightful and unparalleled cause for rejoicing. We should not overlook this opportunity, for although our lives may have lost touch with nature's clock, in our minds we still sense a basic thirst for its necessary rhythms.

For the purpose of our picnic party, the lyrical colouring of this season is expressed by picking up a whole range of greens and pinks that we see issuing forth around us. Yellow, grey- and blue-greens, and soft, muted and strong pinks as seen in the leaves of beech trees, daffodils and irises, the flowers of apple blossom, hyacinths and campions. The blues depicted are from bluebells and scillas, and the yellows are from the many varieties of daffodils, from the brashness of Harvest Gold to the only-just-yellow of Paper Whites. This colouring, which expresses the untainted quality of spring, is particularly transitory, pausing only briefly before evolving into the full-blown brilliance of high summer.

May Day festivals are very much alive in Cornwall and other regions of the country. The festooned streets around the old quay at Padstow still throng with white-clad figures with blue or red neckerchiefs and caps brimming with flowers. Maypoles are erected in many villages where little girls weave around them with bright gala ribbons. We paint colourful stripes down the middle of strips of white sheeting for our ribbons. Pinked with shears and prettily knotted, they make up the required lengths.

with the edge, 46 cm (18 in) from it. This is to form a clear channel in which to print the blossom border. When the checks are complete, this broader tape is removed with the others and the apple blossom border is satisfyingly stencilled down the middle of the blank area. The outer edges of the cloth are also left plain having been masked off with tape to a depth of some 10 cm (4 in). This is scalloped with pinking shears.

A number of 30 cm (12 in) squares of cloth are chequered across on a smaller scale and in various gingham colours. They are to be used as napkins to line the individual picnic baskets. The edges of these napkins are also pinked into scallops, and on to these curves are painted some small extra flowerheads. In order to add to the lacy effect created by the pinked edges, the centre of each flower has been punched out with a paper punch.

I designed two styles of cushions. One is a chequered square with a strip of stencilled border running around the sides to form a gusset. The other one is round, its flat surface encircled with a ring of apple blossom; this time the gusset strip is made up of pink checks. Wine-coloured piping picks up the deep maroon in the centre of the

TABLE LINEN AND CUSHIONS

Having decided to enliven our picnic with streamers made of cloth, I choose several colours from a clutch of cotton ginghams. This is a fabric more generally associated with schoolgirls' frocks. Cut on the cross into lengths, it makes cheap and effective ribboning.

I decide to contrive an enlarged edition of this classic check to be used in conjunction with a stencilled border of apple blossom for a special tablecloth and cushions. Using a basic cream cambric, I start by striping it across with parallel lines of masking tape. This is then sprayed over evenly with bright pink paint. The lines of tapes are removed and more are applied, running straight across at right angles over the newly painted stripes. When the spraying process has been repeated, the tapes are removed and this boldly checked, two-toned pattern revealed.

Before spraying the checks on the tablecloth, I first place a broader masking tape running parallel

blossom flowers, while the characteristic nubbly quality of the applewood twigs are depicted in a rich brown. By stencilling on cotton cambric which has a slightly glazed surface, the colour definition came through clearly, emphasizing the slightest tone.

Taking artistic licence, I have spurned the commonplace green of apple leaves for the grey-blue-green of daffodil leaves, a more appealing shade to use next to the strong sugar-pink checks. Laid out with a disparate collection of flowery china, the tablecloth and cushions add to the prevailing mood of spring fever.

PARTY FARE

More than a century ago, the first Sunday in May saw groups of families banding together and going off into the countryside to picnic. Their destination might well be some neighbouring farm where the farmer was either related or just friendly. Friendly enough to allow his kitchen range to be used to bake the heavy cake, the plain ingredients of which had been brought along. Also, he would allow the milk, still warm from the cow, to be purchased for junket, to the children's delight. The grown-ups would refresh themselves with plenty of tea or, if they were not Methodist, some invigorating rum punch, before they trekked back home to their own cottages, feeling wonderfully exhilarated after having a rare day of being out in the open, doing nothing in the way of work.

For our expedition we have small baskets woven in willow cane, the silky, silver bud of which are already opening; interwoven with the cane are raggy strips of gingham. The children are happily excited about carrying their own food in them to the picnic spot. Pretty china teacups must be carefully balanced as they are set with junket, faintly flavoured with raspberries and sprinkled with brown nutmeg. Chrome yellow saffron buns are a must for any 'tea treat' in this part of the world. Saffron has been in Cornwall since the Phoenicians came trading for tin, and it has always been a treasured ingredient. 'As dear as saffron' is the old expression, still used.

On the cloth spread under the old slanting tree is an array of cakes; a showcase for country

baking, they form the centre of our picnic. Cakes made with caraway seeds, marbled with raspberry juice, chequered Madeira coated in marzipan and an open fruit tart compete for takers. Splits and cream, the star of the legendary West Country cream teas, are so named because they are scones, split in two halves and spread with jam and clotted cream. A fish dish of homemade sardine paste and a curd cheese provide some welcome savoury flavouring.

Making lemonade with fresh lemons, infused with water and vanilla sugar is easy and also very enjoyable as the glorious citrus aroma fills the kitchen. When cooled and strained into a large jug, it makes a delicious outdoor drink.

Sitting on the grass, dotted with petals from the apple blossom, the long-stemmed daisies are picked for making chains. Slit near the end of each stem with the thumb nail, they are slotted through each other to form a continuous chain. Made up into different-sized circles and worn on the head or around the neck or wrist, they make many a little girl feel like the Queen of the May.

One of the Newlyn artists of the last century painted a delightful scene of little girls walking in procession up from the quay. A pretty picture indeed, in their full white pinafores against the background of a china-blue bay. They were on their way to have tea on the lawns of an outlying manor house. The little ones were lifted into wagons to sit on the bales of straw, as the procession wound up the Coombe to the house.

Various amusements are planned for after our tea party, including a paper-chase across fields and through some woods, following a confetti trail laid by a fast 'hare'. Sports in a nearby field include egg-and-spoon, three-legged and wheelbarrow races and many other diversions. Finally, rambling along past hedgerows starred with primroses and under trees, dense at this time with seas of bluebells, paths are taken towards home.

Sheltered by a bank smothered in daisies, the children, sitting on plump cushions in the dappled sunlight, enjoy their picnic tea. A white basket of forget-me-nots is suspended from the tree over the centre of the cloth.

WELL DRESSING

AT THE BEGINNING OF MAY THE ANCIENT HOLY WELLS OF CELTIC CORNWALL
ARE AT THEIR MOST POTENT. THOUGHT TO POSSESS THE POWERS OF HEALING
AND PREDICTION, THEY ARE STILL VISITED AT THIS TIME BY PEOPLE SEEKING
THE BENEFIT OF THEIR GIFTS. DRESSED AS A TRIBUTE IN ALL THE GLORIOUS
WILD FINERY OF THIS MONTH OF FLOWERS, THEIR HUMBLE SETTINGS
ARE TRANSFORMED.

*Crossing the stream at the water-splash by means of huge granite stepping
stones, the children are on their way to the well, which has been decked out
specially for May Day.*

In the furthest corner of a stretch of farmland down the valley from our buildings is a very ancient holy well which is called Alsia, very seriously, for it is wreathed about with legends and folklore. From time immemorial these ancient wells were venerated as a magical source of water, a sacred gift from the earth goddess. This was before the arrival of the early Christians. The special qualities of the wells seemed to have changed from pagan to religious during the period in this country when the Celtic saints, the early Irish missionaries, first landed to establish their monastic supplements in the fifth and sixth centuries AD. One such settlement was our parish of St Buryan. St Beriana was the very beautiful daughter of an Irish king of Donegal. Legend has it that she arrived here with St Patrick, was converted to becoming a nun by St Piran and was subsequently abducted from her cell by an ardent suitor.

It seems that many of the wells were adopted by these romantic Irish saints, and legends of magical properties were transformed into tales of miracles. Eventually small baptisteries were built close by the wells, at which the needs of the growing bands of pilgrims were well tended. Drinking and washing in the water was considered to be a cure for many ills. Alsia well is thought, after all these centuries, still to have particular qualities for the strengthening of weakly children.

There exists to this day a pilgrim's custom of tying cotton rags to the thorn tree that grows by the well. They are said to be associated with the torn garments of a St Audrey, from which the word 'tawdry' is a derivation. These fluttering votive strips of cotton, the prayer rags of modern

MAKING A GARLAND

A GARLANDED WREATH IS SO EASY TO ASSEMBLE THAT, ONCE YOU HAVE TRIED, YOU WILL NEVER WISH TO BUY A RIGIDLY FORMAL, READY-MADE ONE AGAIN.

I START BY CUTTING OUT A STRIP OF CHICKEN WIRE MEASURING 122 x 23 CM (48 x 9 IN) WITH WIRE SNIPPERS AND ROLL IT LENGTHWISE ON TO ITSELF UNTIL I CAN BEND THE CUT WIRES TO LINK THE ROLL TOGETHER. THEN, CURVING IT AROUND IN A CIRCLE, I HOOK TOGETHER THE SHORT ENDS IN THE SAME WAY, TAKING CARE TO KEEP THE ROUNDED SHAPE. THIS PROVIDES THE SKELETON INTO WHICH I PUSH A DENSE MASS OF ROSEMARY SPRIGS TO FLESH OUT THE SHAPE OF THE WREATH. IT IS THEN EASY TO EMBED THE NUBBLY TWIGS OF THE APPLE BLOSSOM REGULARLY AROUND THE RING OF GREENERY.

pilgrims, are carrying on an astonishing tradition that has lasted at least two thousand years.

And so the storytelling can continue as we create a further chapter of springtime celebrations around the well. To make the arches over the entrance gate and the well itself, we buy some of those many-stranded wire supports used for tall flowers in herbaceous borders. Pushing their spiky ends into the ground on both sides, we bend the tops over to meet each other, fastening them with florist's wire. To cover the archway of the gate, we fix masses of branches of blossoming hawthorn with more wire. For the well arch we do the same, but add pink campions, bluebells, forget-me-nots and white lacy cow parsley. This curved concentration of flowers looks almost natural against the fresh green leaves, and grasses.

There is a hauntingly sad story from the last century about the fair daughter of the Miller of Alsia. It tells how Nancy Trenoweth fell for the handsome young son of a well-to-do farmer, Hugh Lanyon, of neighbouring Boscean where she had been sent to work. Before long he also declared his love for her. The Lanyons, however, wished their son Frank to do better for himself than the daughter of the local miller and so sent her off back to her home. Nancy was most unhappy and the pining lovers eventually contrived to meet with the connivance of Nancy's mother. They found the perfect trysting place was the old well beyond the orchards and on this very spot they swore their vows of eternal constancy.

Soon afterwards Frank left to seek his fortune at sea. Nancy moved into the cottage at Alsia and before long, here 'with the sweetest flowers of summer an innocent babe was born into a sinful world'. Some time later a sealed bottle was found on the white sand at Porthcurno, giving news of Frank's capture by pirates in the Bay of Biscay. He did, in fact, escape, but was fatally wrecked off the Cornish coast, only gaining the shore to die at his parents' home before he could set eyes on his beloved Nancy.

Even when they buried him in St Buryan churchyard, she was not told. She did, poor soul, see him that night as an apparition which swept her off on horseback to pull her down into the grave with him, and from this experience she died

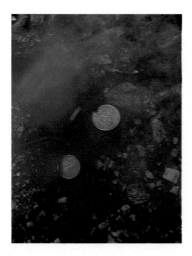

When the children get to the enclosure
around the well, they throw pennies
into the dark recesses of the water,
silently asking, as they do so, for their
secret wishes to be answered. This well
has long been a wishing or divining
well and many small objects have been
thrown into it to see how they land,
how many bubbles rise or how they
turn as they fall to lie on the gravelly
bed beneath the water. Pins, stones or
even floating blackberry leaves are said
to denote a particular course of fate.

of shock. They were then, at last, united in one grave, while their son was left to form a bridge of reconciliation between the two families.

On warm evenings it was said that scores of maidens went and clustered around on the banks by the well, fervently awaiting their turn to toss in some pebbles. They believed the well could define where their paths lay for the future, particularly in affairs of the heart. The first three Wednesdays of May are the days of the year when the well is at its most potent and probably its most beguiling, as all about it the warmer earth is bursting with life.

Before daybreak on the morning of May Day, the young people of the towns would swoop out

A farmer might also offer his barn or a field in which the first music of the day would be struck up to accompany some boisterous reels before the revellers went on their way. Wooden whistles were cut and their shrill sound would announce the bringing-in-the-green, the coming of the May into the town. The church bells of Helston still ring out at six o'clock in the morning on the 8th May to usher in the summer, and the first dance in a day of dancing starts at seven, processing through the garlanded streets accompanied by the town bands. Certain houses of the town have their doors wide open, for they are expecting the dancers to swirl right through the house and out the other side. The ten o'clock dance is for chil-

into the country in order to 'bring home the May'. This harvest of green branches, blossom and spring flowers, mostly bluebells, was collected to decorate the fronts of the houses of the town for the coming day of celebrations. It would seem that if a lad could nail a bough of May blossom above a farmer's door before he was up and about, the farmer was obliged to supply him with a sturdy breakfast. A slice of bread smothered in cream was offered and the slice had to be the length of the longest fern the lad could find. However the hospitality of the farmers did not need to be tricked from them as they gladly offered generous sustenance to all who came. Mead, hedgerow wines and junket were offered, a homely country breakfast, strange to us. It strikes me that the whole episode is possibly the source of the phrase 'junketing around'.

dren and last year I had the joy of watching nine hundred children, all in white, dance through the winding streets of this hillside town. The music of *The Furry Dance* is ancient and monotonous; the word 'furry' is thought to mean a feast or fair.

The power behind these springtime rituals expresses to me how chronically out of touch we are with the forces of nature. If May Day means anything out of the ordinary to most people today, it is a day when trade unions march (not dance) in file through our cities to proclaim their rights. A very far cry from expressing the rites of spring.

Events such as the ones I have briefly recounted – and there are very close parallels to them in many cultures – lie dormant as part of our heritage, and are there to be reclaimed if we should wish to.

CHILDREN'S GARLANDS
THE CHILDREN SIT RESTING AFTER COMPLETING THEIR JOURNEY, A MAY DAY PILGRIMAGE TO THE WELL. THEIR GARLANDS OF GREENERY ARE MADE BY ENTWINING VINE-LIKE BRANCHES TO FORM A RING AROUND THEIR HEADS. TIED WITH WINE-COLOURED RIBBONS TO STOP THEM SLIPPING LOOSE, THEY REST LOW ON THE BROW. GEORGINA HAS BLUEBELLS AND APPLE BLOSSOM TUCKED INTO HERS, WHILE PETER'S IS LEFT PLAIN WITH JUST LEAVES AND THE RIBBON TO SECURE IT.

Summer

WEDDING DAY

A YEAR OR TWO AGO, WHEN PLANNING A FAMILY WEDDING, THE BRIDE EXPRESSED A
STRONG PREFERENCE FOR HAVING THE RECEPTION AT HOME, AN ENCHANTING
ENOUGH SETTING, WITH THE OLD HOUSE AND MILL IN A VALLEY BY A MEANDERING
STREAM. SHE WANTED NOTHING BROUGHT IN OR ORDERED FROM A PROFESSIONAL
SUPPLIER, NOT THE CAKE, NOR THE DRESS, NOR THE PHOTOGRAPHS. EVEN THE CAR
THAT TOOK HER TO THE CHURCH HAD TO BE A FAMILY CAR, DRIVEN BY A RELATION,
FAMILIAR AND REASSURING TO STILL THE COMPLEX FEELINGS OF SUCH A DAY.

*Wide white ribbons and vivid posies decorate the bridal car (left). Refreshing
fruit sorbets sit in a garland of flowers encased in ice. A large bowl of flower-
strewn ice to cool the summer drinks (above).*

Inspirations

It is clear from the colourful selection of inspirational materials that this is not going to be a peach-and-pastel wedding. The chosen scheme that emerges is primary bright blue, true scarlet, golden yellow and a strong green. All have a clarity that is crystal clear against the traditional billows of white. More muted greens represent the garden setting.

On one postcard some young aristocratic ladies, clad in beautiful white Edwardian dresses, tend a symbolic orange tree at Chatsworth, Derbyshire. On another card white blossoms are inscribed across a Persian tile. The connection of orange blossom with wedding days is so delightful as it brings with it the heady scent of its waxy flowers. Other gathered ephemera depicts images of ribbons, rings and hanging flowers.

A portion of ancient, elegantly festooned Roman wall suggests the glimmering of an idea for painted tenting. The whole of this wall is a prime exhibit at the Metropolitan Museum in New York.

Scarlet ricrac and cotton flowerheads underline the notion of a simple clear bright concept. The sky, too, will need to be a Mediterranean blue.

Previously, as a guest at the weddings of a number of contemporaries, the bride-to-be had felt saddened at the way they were all 'of the same mould'. Taken out of the hands of the couple concerned, they were regimented by the caterers, photographers and hire firms. When they are well briefed, some firms take great care to make provision for appealing personal touches; however it is difficult for them to express the precise stylistic nuances of this or that particular family celebration. This is most accurately mirrored through a hotch-potch of detailed references. It does require courage to take the organisation of a wedding in hand yourselves, but proves well worth while on the day.

At the outset you will need to recruit a group of willing helpers, firstly from among the family, young and old; all will be pleased to take an

active part of it. Grandmothers who have done it all before, can expound on particular traditions, and point out many a pitfall. Even the very young can help with tasks like gathering flowers and making them into small posies for the church.

THE CHURCH

The inland church at Sancreed in Cornwall was much loved by the 'plein air' painters of the Newlyn School at the turn of the century. Idyllically set in woodlands, it has a very early interwoven Celtic cross standing by the pathway to its door. This same path must have been strewn with herbs and rushes on many a wedding day in the past, as was the custom long before the days of confetti. Inside it is rich in darkly patterned texture. There are panels of dense carving on the old screen by the altar steps and more on the wooden roofing supports. This dark interior proved an effective foil for the brightness of the flowers decorating it for the ceremony.

Large and rounded bunches of bright flowerheads mark each side of the aisle where the bride and groom first stand. Later at the altar they are flanked by great clouds of yellow roadside flowers, pailfuls of a so-called 'weed' of high summer (left). Smaller posies of the same flowers are lodged between the beams of the ceiling and fill the stone niche in the porch. They are becomingly tied about with scarlet streamers, cut and curled from paper. Geraniums are an unusual choice for a wedding as are yellow ragwort and camomile daisies. However, when they are put together with blue hydrangea heads, they give the impression of exuberant and joyful celebration, which is after all why they are there.

A gateway dressed fit for Madame
Bovary to step from as she progressed
through the garden on her way to her
own wedding. It is hooped with a haze
of yellow and surmounted by a large
rounded ball of mixed flowers
(above). The terrace is hung with a
backdrop of stencilled tenting, which
folds back at the entrance to the
reception room. Here the wedding
breakfast is laid out on colourful
cloths. The guests can stroll in the
garden and sit in convivial groups on
the sun-warmed granite steps.
The humble geraniums in terracotta
flowerpots hold their place of honour
as flower of the day (right).

Stencilled columns form an architectural illusion on the white fabric around the terrace. As I wanted a true white, I chose a cotton twill instead of the more practical choice of canvas, as this is invariably off-white (far right). The centre flaps of the decorated twill are looped elegantly back just enough to form a tent entrance through the open double doors. With the tubs of white hydrangeas placed each side of the steps, the stage is set.

I called on help to place each cut stencil in turn over its marked-out position, and to stencil the designs in brightly coloured spray paints. We worked on the large table in my studio, but a long trestle table could accommodate the length of a pillar (right).

MAKING THE BACKDROP

After taking simple but careful measurements of the terrace area and the exact position of the centre of the door opening (which will cause a necessary divide in the fabric at this point), I ordered the correct amount of cloth. Meanwhile, I carefully drew up the pillar and its linking festoon to the correct scale on stencil card, then I busily set to cutting away the design shapes from the card. Before stencilling, I divided up the cloth and marked out the exact positioning for the pil-

STENCILLED BACKDROP
THERE IS NO NEED TO TRAVEL TO
SOME EXOTIC VENUE OR HIRE AN
ELABORATE MARQUEE FOR THE
WEDDING RECEPTION. THE PLAINEST
AND MOST UNPROMISING VILLAGE
HALL, OR EVEN BACKYARD, CAN BE
DISGUISED WHEN CLOAKED IN
IMPRESSIVE IMAGES ON CLOTH.
EMMINENTLY ADAPTABLE,
DECORATED CLOTH BRINGS ABOUT
AN INSTANT GLAMOROUS
TRANSFORMATION WHEN STRUNG UP
AROUND PERIMETER WALLS. IT IS
NOT EVEN ESSENTIAL TO BUY SPECIAL
FABRIC, AS A PAIR OF WHITE COTTON
SHEETS COULD BE USED TO GREAT
EFFECT.

I DECIDED TO MAKE A
GLAMOROUS BACKDROP FOR THE
SMALL TERRACE WHERE THE COUPLE
COULD RECEIVE THEIR GUESTS AND
GENERALLY GATHER FOR TOASTS
AND SPEECHES IF THE WEATHER WAS
ACCOMMODATING. A FLIMSY MUSLIN
CANOPY WAS ERECTED TO SOFTEN
THE LIGHT RATHER THAN TO
PROTECT AGAINST BAD WEATHER.

lars and festoons with tailor's chalk, making sure that there was a pillar equidistant from each far end of the cloth and at each side of the door.

Once the stencilling was complete and the fabric cut in two at the entrance divide, all eight edges of the two pieces were deeply hemmed around   and

eyelet holes rivetted at intervals of 25cm (10in) into the double thickness of the top hem.

We were then able to hook up our tenting around three sides of the terrace by means of some convenient barge boarding and a few masonry nails driven into the stonework.

WEDDING CAKE

ANYONE CAN DECORATE A SPLENDID
CAKE IF THEY USE THIS VERY
EFFECTIVE IDEA. BRIGHT GREEN
ICING HAS NOT ONLY BEEN USED TO
PIPE A SIMPLE RING AROUND EACH
BASE, BUT ALSO TO DRAW A SERIES
OF LEAFY BUT HEADLESS PLANTS
SPARSELY ALL ACROSS THE SURFACE
OF THE WHITE ICING. THE TOPS OF
THESE ICED STALKS HAVE BEEN
PIERCED WITH A STILETTO AND THE
SHORT STALKS OF REAL FLOWERS
PUSHED STRAIGHT INTO THE HOLES.
POLICEMAN'S BUTTONS, CAMOMILE
DAISIES, RAGWORT AND THE BUDS
OF MORE GERANIUMS PROVIDE THIS
MIXED BAGFUL OF PURE COLOUR. A
SIMPLE AND SATISFYING PROCESS
WHICH MUST BE CARRIED OUT JUST
BEFORE THE CAKE MAKES ITS
APPEARANCE. TO EXTEND THE
HEIGHT, THE CAKE IS TOPPED WITH A
FLUTE OF THE MIXED FLOWERS WHICH
FAN OUT ON LONGER, MORE
DELICATE STALKS. A DENSE RING OF
GERANIUMS TUCKED AROUND THE
BASE CONCLUDES THE DRAMATIC
PRESENTATION OF THIS COLOURFUL
CAKE.

THE WEDDING BREAKFAST

There is an endearing painting by a member of the Newlyn group I mentioned before of a bride in a kitchen of an old cottage, standing in her finery, resplendent for a day. Before her are her admiring relations. It is sentimental to the hilt, but aren't weddings all about that? It brings home to me how, by contrast, these celebrations have now been removed from the family and out into the glossy world of status display. This bride had plenty of help as she dresses in her own room before proceeding to the church ceremony and the subsequent party under the trees of the garden. It was an occasion of family pride, religious solemnity and simple rejoicing. No place for ostentation or over-elaborate food..

The cake that reigned over the table at a wedding breakfast was not always the tower of iced confections we know and expect today. It was originally a simple affair, made purely from wheat or barley, and it depicted the desire of the assembled well-wishers that the couple should be blessed with fertility. Cut into fingers it was symbolically passed through the wedding ring by the attending groomsman. We have cut the cake into fingers to be distributed in baskets by the young bridesmaids, but as we eat it, do we still remember the significance of these portions of bridal cake today?

The tables are covered in cloths as colourful as an American bridal quilt. In fact their inspiration came from that amazing collection of quilts at Claverton Manor, outside Bath (The American Museum). I designed them for a particular celebration there. They display the same formal gaiety as the hangings, and give a clear message that a union is a cause for rejoicing.

On the table are gilded green plates and numerous posies are lined up along the centre of it like miniature multi-coloured bay trees. Rounded napkins are made from thin white interfacing, which is folded and cut with scalloped edges, then stencilled with a ring of flowers. They make pretty linings for the cake baskets, which are also hand-painted with the same motif and trimmed around the handles with red paper streamers.

The wedding breakfast on its colourfully patterned quilt-like cloth is glimpsed between the divided hangings (left).
The cake with its dressing of real flowers sits in a ring of bright red geraniums (above).
Fingers of cake lie in a prettily lined basket of scalloped and stencilled thin white interfacing (below).

PIRATE PARTY

Story-books are full of amazing adventures woven around the dubious deeds of pirates; their antics spell out pure adventure. When children reach the age when the usual party formula of tea and games is too tame, what could raise enthusiasm higher than a boisterous Pirate Party? By the sea or in the backyard, there's fun to be had in every direction.

The sinister skull-and-cross-bones flashes about against the sky whilst the stockade is manned by a particularly menacing pair of pirates. Strident spots and stripes inventively decorate the cups and plates.

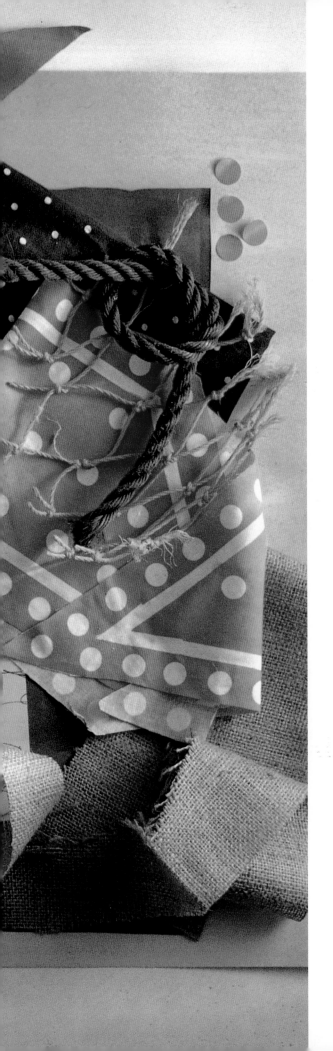

Inspiration

It takes only a little imagination to visualize the coastline around us here in Cornwall as being the habitual haunt of pirates. With a great black barque rakishly anchored in one of the bays, a gang of swarthy men row a long-boat swiftly towards the shore, leaping out where the sea is breaking to pull it up through the soft, pale sand into a cove. Unloading barrels and chests, they hoist them up on to their shoulders and make for some caves at the top of the beach. They shout abuse to each other, brawling and scuffling in the sand before sculling off to bring in more booty before a change in the tide.

Every stage in the land must at some time have shown the trappings of a pirates' lair, whether for a rollicking performance of The Pirates of Penzance or the spine-chilling tale of the Black Spot, with Long John Silver and his parrot. So there is no shortage of visual imagery to draw on for putting together a very colourful party. Flags, kites and costumes can be contrived in scarlet and blue, glinting gold and dense black. Against the ochre of the sand, the black rocks and the raw blue of the sea, this presents an excitingly theatrical mixture. Battered and distressed props are assembled for the den: old boxes, crates, barrels, ropes and lanterns, and a large cage for a mocked-up parrot. The chest which will contain the treasure trove is chosen for its aged look, and maps, bottles, cutlasses and pistols are contrived with an eye to a veneer of antiquity. All that is needed now is a crew of verve and spirit to act out an afternoon of dire deeds, blood and thunder.

Fir poles lashed firmly together to form the platform of the raft (left). Taking her role seriously as a threatening pirate's mate, Alice makes it ashore. Climbing aloft on a make-shift rope ladder to keep a wary eye on what is looming on the horizon (right). A workmanlike model of a lugger becalmed in a rock pool (far right).

Of all the amazing tales of fiction, it is a surprising fact that, when they are compared to a story based on an actual life, this often surpasses them in adventurous content. Such was the life of Henry Carter, one of a family of ten, born near Helston in Cornwall in 1749. Called 'The King of Prussia' for his audacious deeds, he and his family were famous for their smuggling from the hauntingly beautiful inlet, Prussia Cove.

Finding that he could not make a living for himself above the level of 'decent poverty' by working in farming, fishing or mining, in the way his family had always done, Harry turned to smuggling. In this particular far tip of England the general consensus on smuggling at that time, even among the gentry, was that it was not the practice but the law that was wrong. It was said that even the revenue officers 'wore fog specs and banknote shades', and the magistrates themselves

were not blind to the monetary benefits and otherwise of the rich contraband.

Plying his lucrative trade out of Prussia Cove across the wide waters of the English Channel,

young Harry Carter met with uncommon success.

His smuggling adventures led him into battles on sea and shore with Excise men and foreign privateers. Just before the Christmas of 1777, he was aboard his prize sloop off the coast of Guernsey on a smuggling run when his bowsprit parted and he and his crew were forced to put into St Malo for a replacement. Being without proper papers, they were arrested by the customs men, imprisoned in the castle of St Malo and their wonderful cutter was impounded.

In prison Harry had much time to lament his great losses. One night he dreamt that an angel said to him, 'Except thou reform thy life, thou must totally be lost forever.' For a while this pronouncement had a sobering effect, but, on being released with his brother John in exchange for two Frenchmen, he was free to return to his old ways.

Although in the years that followed he married Elizabeth Flindel of Helford and had a little daughter called Betsy, he in no way settled down. One wild sea adventure followed another, even

BUILDING A RAFT

THERE IS PROBABLY AS MUCH FUN TO BE HAD FROM CONSTRUCTING A RAFT AS FROM PUTTING IT TO SEA FOR GAMES. WE PREPARED TEN POLES OF DOUGLAS FIR OF EVEN RATIO IN 1-1.2M (3-4FT) LENGTHS. TAKING THEM DOWN THE SLIPWAY WITH PLENTY OF STRONG ROPE, WE PROCEEDED TO LASH THEM TOGETHER. LAYING SEVEN OF THEM SIDE BY SIDE, SUPPORTED OFF THE GROUND BY TWO SINGLE POLES LYING IN THE OPPOSITE DIRECTION, WE WEAVE THEM EVENLY TOGETHER WITH THE ROPE, CREATING A PLATFORM-LIKE STRUCTURE. SHARPENING ONE END OF THE LAST REMAINING POLES LIKE A GIANT PENCIL, WE THEN FORCED IT BETWEEN TWO OF THE LASHED-TOGETHER POLES TO FORM A MAST. TO KEEP THE MAST VERTICAL, GUY ROPES ARE FIXED TO ITS TOP, THEN STRETCHED OUT AND FASTENED TO EACH CORNER OF THE RAFT. DECKED OUT WITH FLAGS AND FLOATS, THE RAFT IS MADE FAST TO THE SHORE WITH A PAINTER, TIED FIRMLY TO A BOLLARD.

more knife-edged than the last. At one point, customs men caught him red-handed about to loosen the hatches to unload a forbidden cargo. In the débâcle that followed, he was brutally wounded and left for dead. In the dark he crawled to the stern and dropped over the gunnels, almost to die from weakness in the sea. As luck would have it, the tide was with him and it went out fast, allowing him to wade ashore and be rescued.

After this episode, a price was put on his head and he was forced into hiding in a house in Marizion. He spent this time studying navigation,

with occasional visits from his wife and daughter. However, with pressure mounting for his capture, he was forced to leave them and flee the country.

Is it any wonder that, with such real-life romance, there arose such flamboyant legends around the activities of pirates? From the villains of Treasure Island to Daphne du Maurier's sinister inhabitants of Jamaica Inn and her elegant hero of Frenchman's Creek, pirates are synonymous with colourful adventure. Taking the law into their own hands, they ruled the high seas and intimidated landlubbers. I often see in the streets of Penzance swarthy-looking men whose ancestors may well have been numbered among these buccaneers. In fact, there are still some Carters in the district, proud to claim kinship with the infamous captain.

MAKING THE COSTUMES

It is therefore with unabashed colour that we go about dressing our pirates. We stripe white tee-shirts bright red and blue, and spot white cotton scarves in the same colours. We buy sinister black eye patches and large brass curtain rings from chain stores. All heaped in a bag with more scarves, buckled belts, rings and a sponge-bag full of make-up, it is carted to the beach.

To stripe the plain tee-shirts, we lay them out flat over a large piece of newsprint paper. After

sticking three horizontal strips of masking tape edge to edge across the front of one tee-shirt, fastening them on to the newsprint on each side, we pull away the middle strip. This leaves an even, uncovered band of cotton shirting. This is repeated until the whole front of the tee-shirt is striped across with tapes. Then we spray the front of each shirt with either bright red or blue paint. We pull off the tapes when the paint is dry, which doesn't take long, to reveal a set of swashbuckling stripes. The process can then easily be repeated on the back.

It is fun making the spotted scarves. A piece of cotton sheeting is pressed and cut up into a whole variety of scarf shapes, square, long and triangular. Each scarf has a border of masking taped lines framing its shape, just measured in

from the edges. It doesn't matter how far in, as long as it is even.

We use the same system as the tee-shirt stripes, running the tapes along side by side, three at a time to keep them even, then pulling away the middle tape. By using different widths of tapes, we can vary the sizes of the stripes. The dots are also different sizes. Available in different sizes and colours in stationery shops, they are just right for our flamboyant pirate scarves. We press them down in regimented lines between the borders and evenly space them across the central areas. There is great excitement when we peel them off after the paint has dried to reveal crisp clear spots within neat sharp borders.

When the children arrive, scrambling down to the beach in their basic kit of shirts, jeans and gumboots, we set about turning them into a band of ferocious pirates. Bright scarves are flamboyantly knotted around heads, necks, waists and even knees, and gold rings are hooked on to ears with loops of thin cotton. The stripy tee-shirts look marvellous under the paraphernalia of waistcoats, scarves and chains. From a bag of outdated cosmetics, we smear their faces with colour, making barbaric markings across noses, cheeks and chins. Beards, moustaches and heavy brows are drawn on with dark eye pencils and a fetching black patch is placed high on Alice's cheekbone. When some of the children put on the wide black hats which mock the headgear of more respectable seafarers, the whole rakish look comes together well.

Down in the cove at Cape Cornwall where we

Spotted scarves are made of cotton sheeting masked off with sticky paper dots and framed with strips of tape. Clare deftly applies some gruesome markings to the face of a handsome young pirate. A plain white tee-shirt in the process of becoming striped with the aid of masking tape and spray paint (left). Our band of buccaneers waiting outside their hideaway for a likely vessel to hove into sight for them to give chase (above).

are staging our party, there are many small fisherman's huts built into the cliffside from whatever materials come to hand. We are kindly allowed to commandeer one of them, sited right out on a ledge of the cove, for our pirates' hideaway. It is just the job with its thick stone walls and rough black door. We hang the parrot's cage in the doorway and a lantern in the window, but otherwise it contains every convenience for a seafaring life. Nets are strewn inside and out, and crates for carrying fish make good seats and tables. A formal hoisting of the Jolly Roger, the black flag of piracy, over the den seals its authenticity.

TREASURE MAP

IN ORDER TO CONTRIVE A MAP FOR THE TREASURE HUNT WHICH HAS A SUITABLE FEELING OF ANTIQUITY ABOUT IT, WE PHOTOCOPY A VERY OLD MAP, TINTING IT WITH WATERY WASHES OF BROWN INKS TO AGE IT AND TO EMPHASIZE SOME OF THE LETTERING. BECAUSE THE PHOTOCOPY PAPER IS THIN AND WE WANT A FEELING OF THICK PARCHMENT, WE FUSE IT TO A SHEET OF CARTRIDGE PAPER BY SPRAYING THE BACK WITH GLUE. WHEN IT IS FIRMLY STUCK, WE PAINT A LINE OF WATER JUST IN FROM THE EDGE, THEN JAGGEDLY SINGE AROUND THE OUTER EDGE WITH A CIGARETTE LIGHTER, MELTING THE TWO PAPERS TOGETHER. THE LINE OF WATER PREVENTS THE WHOLE THING FROM GOING UP IN FLAMES. ROLLED UP, TIED WITH A BIT OF OLD RED RIBBON AND SEALED WITH RED WAX, THE MAP PRESENTS AN EXCITING PROSPECT.

All hands are needed to launch the raft into the shallow waters of the cove. It spills about a bit, but eventually rights itself as it's secured fast to the shore with a long, strong rope. Great fun is had as various crew take a turn while it is hauled in and out across the water.

There is talk of Spanish treasure and a sealed map is produced, which is zealously read. Plans are laid for an expedition to the cove around the headland. Provisions for all – apples, a few spicy biscuits and bottles of juice – are gathered and tied in spotty napkins to waists and sticks. Armed to the hilt with wooden swords, cutlasses and pistols, and even with one sinister fellow on a

crutch, the party sets off across the rocks.

The adventures that follow are too numerous and blood-curdling to relate. A further clue to the whereabouts of the treasure was found mysteriously in a bottle that washed in on the tide. The raft was used in the rescue of some poor French sailors from the dark hold of a Spanish ship, where they had been manacled since their capture off the coast of Barbary. There are many timber-shivering episodes before the treasure is finally located in a sandy inlet. It is buried beneath the sand in an old barnacled chest and, when finally opened, is full of 'precious jewels'

and coins – the proverbial 'pieces of eight'. Hauling it ashore up the slipway between the boats, the pirates return tired and triumphant.

GAMES AND RACES

After a hearty meal they are ready for more action. Games and races are organized on the slipway. The dressed-up pirates look at their most authentic as they involve themselves in the antics of the various races. Entering in pairs with their inside legs tied together, they hobble up the incline, clutching at each other and falling over like drunken men in their efforts to win the

three-legged race. They are again in pairs for the wheelbarrow race. One of the pirates holds another by his legs, which splay out on each side of him like the handles of a wheelbarrow; pushing himself up on his arms the wheelbarrow progresses forward on his hands. This race is run on a stretch of soft sand to avoid accidents with grazed knees and noses.

For the sack race, each pirate climbs into a sack. Clutching it about him with both hands, he hurls himself forward in leaps and bounds, all the time hampered by the confines of the sack. We prepared sacks especially for this race, to add to the drama of it all and to keep it close to the

party theme. Getting some proper hessian sacks from a farmer, we lay them flat on a table and place a large square stencil of skull-and-crossbones across the bottom portion. It doesn't matter about the top part, as this will be held crumpled against the body. Using a can of matt black paint, we spray it over the cut-away image. This looks like a common trade mark stamped on the sacks; it gives a jolt to see that it is the trade mark of piracy.

For our younger pirates, a sandcastle competition provides excitement of a different nature. Quietly working on their own with spadefuls of sand, they create castles fit for pirate kings from

A mysterious bottle, carrying a message regarding the whereabouts of treasure, floats on the incoming tide. The 'treasure' pouring out of a shell-encrusted chest is made up of coins and jewellery (left). A photocopied map spread out on a rock is distressed by singeing its edges with a lighter (above).

THE PARROT

THE ANCIENT AND INFAMOUS
PARROT OF TREASURE ISLAND FAME,
'CAPTAIN FLINT', WAS NAMED AFTER
THE FEROCIOUS OLD PIRATE 'PASSING
BELIEF IN WICKEDNESS' THAT BURIED
THE ORIGINAL 'PIECES OF EIGHT'. WE
MAKE OUR 'CAPTAIN FLINT' BY
PHOTOCOPYING A BEAUTIFUL
ILLUSTRATION AND ENLARGING IT
TO LIFE-SIZE. AFTER CUTTING
CAREFULLY AROUND THE ENTIRE
PROFILE OF THE BIRD, I PLACE IT ON
TO AN OFFCUT OF PLYWOOD AND
OUTLINE IT IN PENCIL. AFTER IT HAS
BEEN STUCK DOWN WITH SPRAY
MOUNT ON TO THE CUT-AWAY
PLYWOOD, I WASH TINTS OF WATER-
COLOUR OVER THE IMAGE. A
BICYCLE CLIP IS FIXED WITH A GLUE
GUN TO THE CURVED SHAPE OF THE
PARROT'S CLAW. THIS ENABLES IT
TO SIT CONVINCINGLY ON THE
SHOULDER OF A YOUNG PIRATE,
CASTING SINISTER LOOKS WITH ITS
BEADY EYE.

more exotic lands like Turkey or Morocco. Combing the beach with their buckets, they collect up shells, seaweed and bric-a-brac from the tide-line to garnish the parapets.

MAKING PIRATE PROPS

Colourful and legendary pirates 'as callous as the seas they sail on' have been portrayed in many stories, books and films of adventure. The paraphernalia that accompanied their exploits has been plentifully documented. Great galleons are beyond us, but rafts, pistols, cutlasses, crutches, flags, kites, lanterns, parrots and pigtailed hats are not.

Simplified weaponry of rifles, pistols, swords and daggers are made from scraps of wood and broomstick handles nailed together, painted black and embellished with swirls of gold and silver paint. The handles are tightly bound with string. Ragged flags made from sheeting are sprayed with the Jolly Roger stencil and fixed to crudely striped bamboo poles.

PIRATE FOOD

There is nothing in the least bit formal about the food for the Pirate Party. It is on hand for picking up when the action allows, a format that will meet with the approval of the youngsters. Specially colourful paper plates and mugs have been fun to prepare. Working on a theme of spots and stripes, every conceivable variation has been employed. Using both thick and thin felt tip pens in red, blue and black, each plate presents a different face, as shown in the illustration on page 63.

Sausages and drumsticks are cooked up over a fire amongst the rocks. A shallow bowl contains a salad with groups of prepared but unmixed ingredients – small tomatoes, raw carrots, watercress, radishes and crisp lettuce leaves. Earthenware jugs are filled with apple juice. Dished up from a boat, the chocolate cake, decorated with suitable pirate imagery, is accompanied by popular crunchy brandysnaps. Barrels of apples are on hand all afternoon for munching as aids to acting the part.

PIRATE HATS
IT IS CLEAR FROM THE OUTSET OF PLANNING THIS PARTY THAT A BASIC STENCIL OF SKULL-AND-CROSS-BONES WILL COME IN VERY HANDY. WE USE IT TO DECORATE THE CARDBOARD HATS, THE CAKE, THE FLAGS AND THE KITE. THE HATS WE CUT FROM ONE LAYER OF CARDBOARD IN THE CURVACEOUS SHAPE OF OLD-FASHIONED ADMIRALS' HEADGEAR. SPRAYED OVER BLACK AND STENCILLED WITH A WHITE SKULL-AND-CROSS-BONES, THE EDGES ARE TRIMMED WITH UPHOLSTERY BRAIDS, CORDS, FRINGES AND TASSELS. BLACK ELASTIC IS SLOTTED THROUGH PUNCHED-OUT HOLES ON EACH SIDE OF THE HAT TO HOLD IT SECURELY ON THE HEAD THROUGHOUT THE BOISTEROUS GAMES. A SHORT PIGTAIL OF PLAITED BLACK WOOL IS ATTACHED TO THE ELASTIC AT THE BACK OF THE HEAD, TO FALL ON TO THE NECK.

A crock of apples is kept readily to hand, good pirate food for combating the dreaded scurvy. The cut-out parrot scans the horizon from his vantage point – a perch on the shoulder of the young pirate – secured with a bicycle clip (far left). The chocolate party cake, lying in the bottom of a boat with 'pieces of eight', is emblazoned with the skull-and-cross-bones and flanked by rows of brandy-snaps (left). Jolly Roger flags are stuck in the sand as markers, signals for pirates' games (above).

Summer

PRE-THEATRE
PICNIC

ONE OF THE JOYS OF OUR CORNISH SUMMER IS AN OUTING TO THE MINACK THEATRE. BUILT ORGANICALLY INTO THE CLIFFSIDE, THE STAGE IS A LEDGE ABOVE THE SEA. WITH THE BAY AS A BACKDROP OF SUCH NATURAL GRANDEUR, THE EXPERIENCE IS OFTEN MAGICAL, WITH THE ELEMENTS ADDING WHOLEHEARTEDLY TO THE DRAMA.

The evening audience intent on the unfolding drama of not just the play on stage, but also the evening sky (left). A collection of materials that will make up the paraphernalia of our stagy picnic (above).

It took the amazing vision of a young woman, educated genteelly at Cheltenham Ladies' College, to come down to this corner of Cornwall and create, with her bare hands, this remarkably ambitious cliffside theatre. Rowena Cade, the daughter of a Derbyshire mill owner, whose great-grandfather had been a painter of the Industrial Revolution, must be one of the most unsung talents of her time. Working with the most unlikely tool, a screwdriver, she created the most assured and apt designs driven out of semi-set concrete. It was not just in the detailing that she knew what she was handling; the concept as a whole displays an unusual degree of understanding of how to deal with space inventively. When she involved herself with productions, designing costumes, her talents in this area shone through to the same impressive standard.

Having such an overtly romantic ambience, it was no wonder that the Minack attracted the great film-makers of the 1940s. I remember as a child watching an impassioned Margaret Lockwood playing 'Cornish Rhapsody' on a grand piano set on this same cliffside stage. I was watching a film called Love Story.

Gaunt and white-headed, I recall Miss Cade's

modest, but meticulous figure as she moved across her terrain with the ease of a mountain goat, tending sprucely to its upkeep. She would then have been nearing ninety.

An invitation to join a picnic lunch party for a matinée performance at the Minack should not be resisted. Climbing down to find the seats, carrying the picnic tackle, is exciting, but needs a bit of organization. I have devised, after many years of complicated manoeuvring, an ad hoc system similar to that on airliners. Shallow wooden greengrocer's crates are brought into service. Having been sprayed over roughly in white, a crisp wave is then stencilled around them. Inside, they have been lined with blue polythene cut from dustbin bags to render them waterproof as a guard against spills.

When the food is arranged on plastic dishes, complete with napkins and cutlery, the crates are stacked up and secured with a canvas strap.

Wine and fruit are carried in separate baskets

to spread the load. Disposable plastic wine glasses are spattered on the outside with gradations of blue paint, fading to nothing near the rims. This gives them a fresh fizzy look and ties them in with the other plastic utensils. The bright blue bowls with gentle scalloped edges were given to me when I admired them at The Women's Art School in Delhi; they mix their paints in them. The plates came from France and the cutlery is Italian. For this particular lunch party I decide to fill the dishes with vividly coloured food: red salad and crab, and small, individual summer puddings.

We also choose to decorate our special cushions with very deep edging by giving them the 'Hokusai' wave as a border; extra borders of knotted rope frame a central shell motif. We have also stencilled the umbrella and the canvas backing of a plaid rug, brought with us in case the weather changes for the worse as it so quickly can in sea-lying areas.

The sea design that is stencilled on the cushions in bright blue paint, with the crests of the waves tipped with gold. Ripe peaches and cherries nestle in a basket with some seaside weed. One of the supper trays set with plastic plates and cutlery, with the prepared dishes already served (far left). The picnic lunch strewn along the uniquely decorated seating prior to the performance (above). The essential umbrella, a precaution against rain or strong sun, is stencilled with shells and rope (left).

GARDEN FÊTE

RURAL LIFE IN SUMMER WOULD NOT BE COMPLETE WITHOUT THAT SOCIAL EVENT OF FOND MEMORY – THE COUNTRY FÊTE. NOWADAYS THESE ARE OFTEN RATHER TAME, GENTEEL AFFAIRS AND, WHILE I LOVE THEIR COSY TRADITIONAL FORMULA, I FEEL THEY WOULD BENEFIT FROM BEING INJECTED WITH MORE COLOUR AND THEATRICALITY. SOME SELECTIVE BORROWING FROM THE BRASH GAIETY OF FAIRGROUND BOOTHS, WHICH VIE FOR ATTENTION WITH CLASHING COLOURS AND SOUNDS, MIGHT BE IN ORDER.

The garden stall, with its vivid green and red colour scheme, is brimming over with plants and herbs of all kinds. Greengrocer's fruit boxes and flowerpots are exuberantly decorated with painted designs.

Inspiration

The summer fête is a very British institution. As it is strangely indicative of our rather too controlled sense of fun, I am keen to jazz it up a little, so when I start to visualize the various stalls, I plan strong, bright colours and lively imagery. For the plant stall I envisage the powerful combination of emerald green, scarlet and cerise, with the addition of the grass green of the natural leaves and the brilliant colouring of summer geraniums. The White Elephant stall is to be decked out in indigo blue, crimson, puce and yellow ochre, a group of exotically rich colours associated with India. The 'clean as a whistle' colours for the cake stall are depicted in Dutch blue, white, cream and sugar pink, while the clownish Aunt Sally is a collage of bright circus colours - red, black, yellow and saxe blue. More muted colours are picked to create the bunting flags, the soft colours of English prints, gentle blues and pinks, pale greens and yellows.

The structure of each stall is basically the same. Trestle tables are unfolded and set upon the grass. Set over them is a simple wooden structure, a three-dimensional oblong rather like a single four-poster bed made up from 5 x 5 cm (2 x 2 in) timbers to support the canopies.

Many influences are used to draw attention to our diverse attractions. When recently in India, I loved the garish puppet booths like small tented stages glistening with silks and sequins. The striped stalls of our Punch-and-Judy shows offer an arresting display, while, on a grander scale, the glorious old-fashioned circus tent provides a gala backdrop for the performance. Borrowing a little from these practised showmen, we can put on a fine display. Banishing the yellowing polythene, faded seersucker tablecloths, drab sheeting and cardboard boxes, we set up stalls to be proud of.

Different varieties of plants and herbs spill over from their trays made of fruit boxes. A garden chair and Panama hat are provided for the person manning the stall (above). The decoration on the trowel is hand-painted on to the curve of the metal (below). Terracotta flowerpots are freely painted in bright Mexican colours (above right). A watering can and garden sieve are transformed with a stencil of leaves and flowers (below right).

GARDEN STALL

The glorious colouring of the plants on the garden stall, a diverse collection of flowers, herbs, cuttings and seedlings, lends itself well to some joyful treatment. Vivid emphasis is added with a shaped embroidered door hanging used to frame the front of the structure; this adds the drama of some exotic garden pavilion.

Ever since my first camping expeditions, before the advent of easy nylon, jade green tenting canvas has appealed to me. So sympathetic out-of-doors, it is the ideal material to use for the cladding of this stall, and it provides a brilliant foil for the potted geraniums. Strips of trellis, stained bright green, are tacked on to the upright wooden posts at each side of the trestle table. These are for tying up gardening gloves, tools and strings of flowerpots, all as bright and painted as possible.

Plant trays are made from shallow fruit boxes used by greengrocers. These are painted green and roughly stencilled with leaves. Lined up along the table-top, they make smart compart-ments for the different varieties of plants. They can easily be lifted off the table for watering if it is a scorching afternoon and the plants begin to wilt. They also make a nice extra for carrying the purchased plants away.

Sprayed basic dark green, a galvanized water-ing-can is stencilled with leaves and bright red flowers. An ordinary standard model, it has its shiny brass rose removed before it is sprayed with several coats of enamel paint. Its galvanized inte-rior is left unpainted. A leafy stencil is wrapped around it at two levels and sprayed with different greens. A large peony flowerhead and a small pink are sprayed an unlikely bright red to stand out boldly. A plastic garden sieve is given a more dis-tinguished look with the same dark green base. However, this time the leaves and berries that embellish it have been painted by hand, as the rim is ridged and not flat enough to take a stencil.

A pair of anaemic white tubs are subjected to a tough coat of green enamel paint, then finally dragged with emulsion to simulate wood grain. Scarlet paint is used for the bands. Lengths of thick rope are glued around the inside of each rim to give them a bulkier appearance. Planted with bushy hydrangeas, they look fine.

More paint is used to revive two chipped enamel buckets. We have spattered them all over to cover their chips and cracks by utilizing the clogged nozzles of enamel spray paints. When the buckets are filled with masses of cut flowers, the colours fuse amiably together.

When one thinks of cut flowers it would seem that there are almost two separate species - those blooms grown for presentation bouquets from florist shops and those sometimes ragged and far from perfect flowers that make up the mixture of bunches picked from somebody's garden. The latter, never the same from one week to another, a joy to receive. They are a reflection of personal preferences and amateur skills. The same can be said of all the offerings on our garden stall, cuttings, seedlings, and generously divided plants. They will all readily find themselves new plots in which to flourish in this amiable market exchange.

PAINTED FLOWERPOTS
A BATCH OF TERRACOTTA FLOWERPOTS IS CRUDELY DECORATED BY BEING DAUBED WITH CHILDREN'S POSTER PAINTS, STRAIGHT FROM THE POT WITH NO MIXING. A PLAIN COLOUR IS APPLIED TO THE BODY OF THE POT, LEAVING A SCALLOPED SHAPED BORDER UNPAINTED UNDER EACH RIM. THIS IS THEN DOTTED WITH ANOTHER COLOUR. A VARIETY OF FLOWERHEADS AND LEAVES ARE FREELY PAINTED AROUND THE POT OVER THE BASE COLOUR.

The cake stall is draped with variously patterned cloths in soft confectioner's colours (above). We can't resist the pink icing on these fairy cakes, which emphasizes the yellow of the Cornish saffron buns next to them (right).

HOME-MADE CAKE STALL

With its freshly baked cakes and biscuits, and its jams, marmalades and local honey, the home produce stall is always a major attraction at a country fête. Our stall is as fresh and wholesome-looking as its produce. With its gingham, candy stripes and lacy cake stands, it is a far cry from the all-too-usual scene – food displayed in greying polythene containers and beautiful preserves sadly potted and capped with greaseproof paper and elastic bands.

I have clad the basic structure of the cake stall in suitably domestic fabrics: a pair of striped pink-and-blue curtains, some pink checked drying-up cloths, a half-curtain with lacy white houses and a fine white tablecloth. All are strategically positioned about the stall to protect the produce and draw attention to it. Further attention is attracted by the fluttering paper windmills and the decorative strings of dried apple rings. its style recalls early American households, at least the cinema's romantic versions of them, when all is apple pie and gingham bandbox fresh and candy striped. Pots of home-made preserves, topped with decorative caps, are lined up along a high shelf so that the light can glow through them. Honey is decanted into little china pots in the shape of bee hives to join them on the shelf. At this amateur level of selling such touches are much appreciated.

Every household has a favourite recipe, often passed down from mother to daughter. Cakes such as these are unobtainable commercially and are seized upon at a fête like long-lost friends. If many hands are called upon to set to and bake, the stall can be laden with inviting goodies, tarts and buns, traditional cakes and open fresh fruit flans, and a basket of the gingerbread men that are always popular with children.

are cut out bigger than the cake bases and folded into many segments. These then have small petal-like shapes cut out from them through all the layers. Opened up, they become crudely cut home-made doilies fit for a pantomime. We cut some shelf edging in the same way. This gives the whole stall a pretty, exaggerated, unity, which perfectly sets off the produce, tempting every passerby to try the wares.

MAKING THE CAKE STANDS

The home-made cakes and produce are displayed on doily-trimmed stands which look quite grand but are easy to make. Narrow white tubes (as used for postage) form the stem. With masking tape wound around them in a spiral, they are sprayed a bright sugary pink. The tape is then removed and the tubes are cut up into three different lengths, i.e. 10 cm (4 in), 15 cm (6 in) and 20 cm (8 in). Silvery cardboard commercial cake bases, both square and round, are firmly suck on to the tops of these tubes, and smaller discs of cardboard on to the bottom.

Rounds of thin white paper, such as newsprint,

SETTING UP THE CAKE STALL

Of all the stalls at the fête, the cake stall can most benefit from an overall dress rehearsal. The produce, mostly baked on the day, will only appear at the last moment, so careful planning is required for that extra professional look.

We set up a trestle table in the studio, surrounded by the framework structure, complete with wooden lattice panels on each side. We fix in a wooden shelf for the jams, using small angle irons to secure it to the main structure. A dowelling rod to carry the net curtain that backs the display is slotted on to cup hooks. Next, the stall is dressed-up in its various cloths which are

secured with either drawing pins or a staple gun. The paper windmills are positioned along the top of the frame, where they will flutter in the wind and attract attention. Rings of dried apples are then knotted at intervals along a length of string as if they are still being processed. They are purely decorative, making a symbolic festoon.

The decorated cake stands are positioned on the table with the highest in the back row and the shallow ones in the foreground; some are stacked one above the other. The cut paper frill to line the shelf is glued down into position, so that it does not blow away as the produce is sold. Shallow oblong baskets which will hold the gingerbread, brandysnaps, and shortbreads are also lined with doilies specially cut for them.

We also give some forethought to the process of selling the produce. Tongs and spoons are needed for handling the food, and adequate containers to put it in when sold. We have our smart boxes, but paper bags are also required for the biscuits and sweets. These are tied together on a string and stapled to the back of the table.

The ground-length covering of canvas over the table hides a roomy space underneath for extra supplies as the cakes on display sell out. Here, out of sight, it makes sense to have a few cardboard boxes to separate the different categories of cakes and breads, jams and honey, sweets and biscuits.

Rough corners have now been ironed out, and 'out-of-the-blue' dramas eliminated. A well-groomed face can be presented to the public, a fine display. With many volunteer home bakers producing their best, the stall will be rich in quality as well as variety. All that is now needed is for them to arrive with their separate batches on time.

Cakes are the stars of the show, representing a host of flavours and textures. They vie with each other with their variously decorated tops, from the glossily iced variety with crystallized cherries to the more subtle, sprinkled with caramelized sugar granules. The best of the bunch, the one with the most overt appeal, is kept back from the sale, and is the subject of another guessing game. This time it's the correct weight that is to be judged, and a ticket is bought for each guess.

Old-fashioned summer puddings are made and sold in their bowls, ready to turn out and serve.

They are capped with cotton cloths stencilled with fruits denoting their dominant flavour. Miniature shopping baskets hold home-made fudge, made in batches and chopped into cubes; a cone of paper can be offered filled with a variety of flavours, chocolate, rum, brazil nut and vanilla. There are also stripy cubes of pink-and-white coconut ice. Among the selected breads are loaves dotted with dark currants like Dalmatian dogs and scones for the famous Cornish teas.

HOME-MADE PRODUCE

In these days of instant foods 'out of the packet and on to the plate' and the fading of the practice of sitting down to family meals, the art of real home cooking is in danger of dying out.

We are very good at creating a spectacular dish for the occasional supper party, but simpler more homely recipes are now seldom produced. As this category of food becomes rare, it is the nature of things that it will become more highly valued, and in the end sought after.

A new age of young people are already responding by falling on the home-made produce of these stands, to relish the tastes of the old cooking methods. The result is that grannies are being pestered for newly prized recipes of cakes and jams that for years were thought of as common place. The kind of cooking that was practised in most of the kitchens of the land, with hardly a glance at the recipe books. Great cauldrons of jam bubbling with the fruit of the season, would fill these kitchens with their scent. Jam jars kept from year to year sterilized and lined up along the draining board to be once again decanted and labelled as the new vintage. Titled in a language of the hedgerows, 'Rowan', 'Rosehip', 'Bramble' and 'Crabapple' jellies, 'Damson cheese' and 'Apple butter' were scrawled on the labels in spidery writing. All the fruits of the orchard went into 'Dumpsideary' jam and the delicious elderflower infused the gooseberry jam with a flavour of wine, while marrow jam was frisked up with grated ginger.

These special conserves of summer are the real prizes still to be found and carried off at the midsummer Garden Fête.

CAKE BOXES
I CUT OUT A LARGE LACY DOILY
FROM FOLDED NEWSPRINT AND USE IT
AS A STENCIL TO DECORATE
STANDARD GOLD CAKE BOXES. I
SPRAY OVER THE CUT-AWAY
PATTERN FIRST WITH WHITE PAINT
AND THEN ADD SOFTENING PINK
CENTRES THROUGH A SIMPLE SMALL
ROUND STENCIL. WHEN THE BOXES
ARE FOLDED INTO SHAPE AND TIED
WITH WIDE BAKERY RIBBONS, THEY
LOOK REALLY CHIC.

Gold cake boxes are glamorized for the event with a stencilled pattern and home-made lace cut out of plain newsprint is our effective and cheap method of dressing up the produce (far left). Shallow baskets display home-baked biscuits and gingerbread men. Strings of dried apple rings festoon the front of the stall (left).

WHITE ELEPHANT STALL

The White Elephant stall acts as a magnet to lovers of bric-a-brac who are always on the look-out for a bargain among other people's discarded possessions. The curious name 'White Elephant' comes from a story from the Far East. According to this, the kings of Siam used to present a rare albino 'white' elephant to any courtier with whom they were particularly displeased, as they knew that this animal would prove to be pro-hibitively expensive to keep and would lead to the courtier's ruin.

With that Far Eastern tale in mind, I have used Indian trappings to create the mood for the unex-pected delights of the White Elephant stall. The embroidered hanging around the top of the stall is authentic, while the table is trimmed with a pastiche we made of it with cut-out felt shapes. The long strip of embroidered Indian cloth forms a deeply castellated pelmet around the top of the stall, turning it into a little pavilion. To balance this hanging, a length of sail canvas is cut with a similarly shaped edge. Narrow strips of red felt are stuck along this edge, and other felt shapes – palms and flower heads – are cut out and glued in position. To give the border more texture, the pendant shapes are tied half-way down to form crude cloth tassels. It is then hung at the front of the trestle table on top of an overall cover of plain canvas. A length of colourful old tasselling is attached along the edge of the table to give the finishing touch.

As a child, I always looked for the elephant on the White Elephant stall; a child will not be dis-appointed here, for there is a resplendent creature on the richly coloured panel which forms the back of the stall. It is created from a photocopy of an Indian textile. The blown-up black-and-white image is pasted on to hardboard and coloured in with brushes loaded with brilliant Indian inks. These colours deepen as the whole board is var-nished to make it waterproof.

On the stall miscellaneous objects vie for attention, some contrived, some as found. We decorate a number of large wooden trinket boxes, fitted with trays inside. Their surfaces are painted with vinegar work, where the acidic vinegar

forms a mottled resist in the paint, and they are lined inside with exotic fabrics. I stencil over their painted tops and fronts with patterns of a suitable scale and subject. Many small items are given some added hand-painted decoration to enliven them. Rag dolls, china figurines and stuffed animals complete the mélange.

A childish guessing game is centred around the rag doll. Her name is chosen, Chloë, and secretly sealed up in an envelope. Guess the name cor-rectly and she's yours, a most exciting prospect for a little one to be the lucky winner. Another guessing quiz for those with no interest in dolls is 'How many sweets in a jar'. A prettily stoppered glass storage jar is full to the brim with Dolly Mixture. The nearest guess when the sweets are taken out and counted takes the whole jarful home to share with the family.

Many small wooden or china items can be enhanced or revitalized by hand-painted or stencilled decoration (above). The White Elephant stall with its richly coloured and lavishly decorated trappings.

MAKING MOSAIC FLOWERPOTS

An ingenious way to transform an old terracotta flowerpot into a decorative item is to cover it with tiny fragments of patterned china. Particular satisfaction can be derived from salvaging smashed crockery and putting it to use in this way. After some sad incident, trying to piece together a much-loved shattered object is seldom rewarding even when the bits can be found. Professional mending is only worthwhile if the piece is really valuable.

I now keep a sentimental drawer full of shattered crockery and feel less upset after an accident. Knowing that the pieces will be reclaimed to enliven some plain object with a wild patchwork of china is something of a consolation. The whole process is so pleasing that I have found another source of broken china. Whenever I am on a town beach, an old track through a village or, indeed, just digging in my own garden, I keep an eagle eye open, hoping to glean a prized fragment from sand or soil. The ones I find on the sea-washed beaches have their edges worn beautifully smooth. Patterned pieces are particularly prized and can sometimes be roughly dated, which also adds interest. Just as the oddments of cloth in a home-made patchwork quilt can jog the memory and remind us of times past, so too can these colourful chippings as they are embedded in their thick cushion of soft Polyfilla. Matching and mismatching their patterns and colours, is also a positive pleasure.

In order to cover a flowerpot, make sure you have a good selection of broken ceramic pieces in different shapes and colours. It's tough, at first, smashing them into manageable bits, but they are about to be reincarnated. Mix up a bowl of Polyfilla to a soft consistence and cover the flowerpot with a thick layer of it, up to the rim. While it is still soft, push in the fragments of china to make a pleasing pattern, then leave the Polyfilla to harden.

PAINTING CHINA

Brightly painted crockery is more likely to attract buyers to your stall than tired-looking pastels or white and it is not difficult to create these exotic patterns if you have access to a kiln and a fairly steady hand. For those who are not so adept with a paintbrush, stencilled designs are a successful alternative.

The pretty china cups, sauces and plates have been painted with a variety of flowery patterns. Originally designed for printed textiles, they look well converted on to china. I have always liked all-over patterns on china, seeing the whole design travel across the undulating surfaces to come to an abrupt halt when it reaches the edge of a piece. The scale of the pattern is unexpectedly large and this works well, giving it a fresh new feel. I also like the quality imbued by the brush strikes, which is akin to the broken surface of a wall with a painted finish applied across it.

By working from antique textiles, many beautiful patterns can be revived and live to see another day. With easy access to china paints, this presents plenty of scope for enjoyment. Worked on winter evenings, a great showing could be made at the following summer's fête.

A flowerpot is given a new image with fragments of broken china pushed into Polyfilla to create a bizarre pattern (above). Designs from printed textiles old and new are hand-painted on to plain china plates, cups and saucers (middle). The exotic pattern on this border is made up from pieces of felt and aged tasselling (below). The White Elephant itself, brilliantly coloured with Indian inks (left).

AUNT SALLY

In her traditional form, the Aunt Sally is a portrayal of a large blousy lady with a wide open mouth, into which the young tearaways of the village throw coloured balls with as much accuracy as they can muster. Our Aunt Sally is, in fact, a gaudy clown first visualized by my oldest daughter in her schooldays for our local fête in Gloucestershire. To reproduce it here, we first map it out in charcoal on sailcloth. The large shapes are filled in with a collage of paper or coloured fabric, and it is then worked on some

youngest children to stand closer to the target when aiming their shots. The brilliant face of Aunt Sally represents more than a children's game; it provides a wonderfully wild image that will enliven any event. At the end of the day, it can be rolled up and stored with its poles and balls. Offered on loan to the organizers of any kind of outdoor event, it will be gladly accepted as it is bound to score a hit.

The stalls of our fête are dotted around in Morrab Gardens, which is in the heart of Penzance overlooked by terraces of Georgian houses. Planted lushly in Victorian times, it sports an

In the park small boys try their hand at scoring with 'Aunt Sally'; side flaps prevent the balls from going too far astray (above). At work in the studio, marking out the collaged face of the clown with charcoal, paint and pieces of colourful cloth and paper (right). A child retrieves his ball from the wide open mouth of the startled canvas clown (far right).

more with paints and pens. Finally, the great mouth is cut away and the raw edges reinforced with cord stuck around it.

The main image is flanked by canvas wings on each side to fend off stray balls from passers-by. These wings are decorated boldly in similar vein with stripes and scallops. The whole canvas is erected with the aid of poles and guy-ropes and festooned with home-made bunting.

A basket is placed to one side to contain a dozen or so cheerful rubber balls; prettily marbled, they match the colours of the clown. Graded lines are marked out on the grass to allow the

elaborate cast-iron bandstand and fountain. The sub-tropical plant life flourishes there and makes an exotic backdrop for our planned festivities. To set the mood and attract passers-by, the entrance to the park is garlanded with bunting. An overhead banner explains what the fête is in aid of - it might be to raise money to shore up the church tower or to purchase equipment for the local playgroup. As a traditional accompaniment to such proceedings, the Penzance Silver Band gleamingly turns out to play rumbustiously. The sea is glimpsed just over the pine tops; the scene is set for a happy afternoon.

HOME-MADE BUNTING
THIS IS MADE OUT OF ODDMENTS OF
PRINTED CLOTH IN PRETTY COLOURS.
CUT UP INTO LONG TRIANGLES,
THEY ARE SPACED OUT AT REGULAR
INTERVALS ALONG THE LENGTH OF
SOME STRONG TWINE. THE SHORTEST
SIDE OF EACH TRIANGLE IS THEN
FOLDED OVER AND GLUED DOWN
OVER THE TWINE. THIS IS AN
EXTREMELY SIMPLE EXERCISE, AND
LONG LENGTHS OF FLAGGING ARE
QUICKLY MADE UP. CAREFULLY
STORED SO THAT THE TWINE DOES
NOT GET INTO A TANGLE, IT CAN BE
BROUGHT OUT WHENEVER THERE IS
SOMETHING TO CELEBRATE.

Summer

CARNIVAL

SHROVE TUESDAY WAS TRADITIONALLY A DAY FOR CARNIVALS, A GOOD
OPPORTUNITY FOR A 'LAST FLING' BEFORE THE LENTEN FASTING. NOWADAYS,
IN THIS PART OF THE WORLD, THEY TEND TO BE SUMMERTIME AFFAIRS. THERE
IS HARDLY A VILLAGE THAT WILL NOT GET ITS ACT TOGETHER AND, WITH A
GREAT SENSE OF COMMUNITY, DISPLAY ITS VILLAGE PRIDE.

*A maquette of our tableau, compiled from the work of the painter Botticelli
(left). A three-panel screen is covered with the images mounted on to canvas
(above left). Cotton flowerheads emphasize the patterning of 'mille fleurs' on
the gown (above right).*

Inspiration

Once the decision has been made to enter a float for Mousehole carnival, it is then a matter of choosing a suitable theme. I take an ambitious look at that all-time master of decorative classical imagery, Botticelli, and find in his delicate and delightful 'Venus' a suitable icon of the sea.

Later I read to my astonishment that The Birth of Venus was, it seems, most likely to have been created as a subject for a float for one of the many splendid pageants that were popular in Florence at the time of the great Medicis. Lorenzo de Medici followed his father Cosmo as the head of this ruling Florentine family. Rich and powerful, they were famous for their cultured patronage of the arts, which in part gave rise to the flowering of the Italian Renaissance. Botticelli, among other celebrated artists of this charmed circle, would have been involved in designing the costumes, scenery and floats for these most magnificent of processions.

It seems these pageants became such overt expressions of powerful grandeur that they were thought to be ungodly, even pagan, with their classical themes. A savage opponent of them, Savonarola preached so frantically against them that great bonfires were made on to which the Florentines heaped their so-called 'vanities'. In such a way many of the glories of these great Renaissance artists were destroyed; paintings, furniture, rich costumes and jewels perished on these fires, vanishing forever as a source of intense pleasure.

From this gorgeous painting of Venus, we can only pick up wisps of the impression it must have made. For it depicts Beauty, no less, entering the world on a shell, floating ashore over a crystal sea. Showers of pale roses scatter in the wind blown by the wind-gods, as a wood nymph stands on shore waiting with an enveloping cloak.

MAKING THE FLOAT

Working from black-and-white photocopies of three Botticelli paintings, it is possible to fuse them together. We have to reverse the copied image of one of the goddesses to have her facing the right way towards the central figure of Venus. It takes another, more strenuous session with the photocopier to enlarge the assembled sheets so that the figures are life-sized. Careful coding with letters on the back of each portion prevents this task from getting out of hand. When each section is glued into place, the whole image makes a formidable sight laid out on and nearly covering my studio floor. With months in hand, colouring in this celebrated painting would be an intriguing academic exercise; however, realistically, we have little more than a day, so set about it using pots of poster paint with alarming irreverence. After a great deal of random panache we eventually call a halt, being mildly pleased with the effect of the sea from a distance.

In order to animate our float, our plan is to cut away the oval face of Venus and the two goddesses and to substitute real faces. The design, therefore, takes the form of one large panel with two side flaps, which will conceal the 'mortal' bodies of the players. This shallow box will be secured behind the cab of the truck that will transport the tableau. It may be necessary to construct a shallow platform so that the faces can reach the cut-away shapes.

Before buying the canvas on to which the whole design is to be mounted, it is essential to know some of the measurements of the truck to help calculate the final size of the panels. The breadth across its loading area is pertinent for the main panel. Our local sailmaker supplies us with lovely broad canvas, but it could be joined by machine if not wide enough. When the painted paper is completely dry, we glue it firmly on to the measured-out canvas.

SHELL STENCILS
WORKING WITH SHELLS TO CREATE PATTERNS WITH ENCRUSTED TEXTURES, SUCH AS THOSE TO BE SEEN IN A REMARKABLE SHELL HOUSE NEAR EXMOUTH, USED TO BE A SUITABLE PASTIME FOR YOUNG LADIES. NOT ONLY ROOMS, BUT PICTURESQUE GROTTOS HAD THEIR WALLS METICULOUSLY DECORATED. WITH THE AID OF STENCILS, I HAVE INTERPRETED SOMETHING OF THIS QUALITY ON TO CANVAS. ARRANGING SHELL SHAPES INTO CLOSE PATTERNS INTERSPERSED WITH PANELS OF 'LEAF' SPRAYS, I HAVE ADDED A WATERY GREEN TO THEIR NATURAL COLOURING OF BEIGE, STONE AND PINK. WE USED THIS CANVAS TO COVER THE ROUGH SIDES OF THE TRUCK, BUT IT COULD LOOK VERY PRETTY, FOR INSTANCE, AS A PELMET FOR SOME BATHROOM CURTAINING.

Once the glue is dry, the canvas holding the images is then stretched across three frames made of wooden battens. These panels are secured together so that they stand firmly upright. The paper surface now needs a rich coating of tinted varnish, both to give an antique finish and to make it weatherproof. The rough edging has braid glued around it adding the suggestion of costly and ornate framing.

Erected on a lorry surrounded by swaying branches cut from an ash tree, it is swathed in streamers. Artificial roses and flowerheads are stuck strategically on to the dry varnished surface. With faces displayed like a fairground attraction, the float is greeted with whoops of delight. Some small boys think it's a bit rude, and some of the older people don't quite approve – a little too pagan perhaps.

A pink seashell is placed in a watery corner of the float. The face has been cut away from the tableau and Kate stands behind on a platform to replace it (left). A panel of 'shellwork' stencilled on a canvas apron that we made to hang around the edge of the truck like a cuff. The nymph in her dress of woodland flowers, painted in over the life-sized image (above).

Summer

BEACH PARTY

BEACH PARTIES ARE ONE OF THE MOST RELAXED FORMS OF CELEBRATION. ALL FORMALITY IS BROKEN DOWN AS PEOPLE EAT, DRINK, SIT OR SWIM AS THE MOOD TAKES THEM. IN OUR PART OF THE WORLD, THE VERY TOE OF THE WEST COUNTRY, ARRANGING SUCH AN EVENT IS PARTICULARLY EASY WITH A GREAT DIVERSITY OF HAUNTINGLY BEAUTIFUL BAYS AND INLETS TO CHOOSE FROM. HOWEVER, ANY BEACH, RIVERSIDE OR LAKE CAN PROVIDE A SIMILARLY RELAXED AND BEGUILING SETTING.

Chosen with an eye to its exotic colouring, the food – red mullet, melons and salad – mirrors the resplendent sunset (left). A paper kite and an ad hoc beachcomber's throne (above).

Inspiration

In true beachcomber fashion I start my planning for the
party by gathering and selecting scraps of colours and
textures that will enhance the setting. The aim is to play up
with artifice qualities that are intrinsically present in Nature's
grand sweep of a bay – the chosen spot.

The palette that emerges for this event includes rich sandy
ochres and corals, vibrant turquoise, saxe blue and
aquamarine and a subtle very pale beige, the colour of
washed-out hemp.

The exciting tumble of textures found in flotsam and
jetsam strewn along the tide's edge provides further
inspiration for the party. Pale shanks of driftwood, plastics,
nylon ropes, seaweed and shells are all materials at hand for
recycling into party paraphernalia.

Other materials brought into play are natural textiles such
as cotton, canvas, muslin and towelling, also the woven
basketry of cane and leaves.

SETTING

The terrace of a cafe deserted in the evenings is requisitioned and dressed up. The cardboard cut-out palm trees are fixed to an existing ironwork structure alongside woven panels of matting. This makes a flimsy and evocative shelter.

The utilitarian table is covered with a coral-patterned cotton cloth. (A makeshift table could be erected by utilizing two oil drums, painted around their ridged sides in colourful stripes. These could form supports for a couple of broad planks.) Pretty raw silk cushions stencilled with a fan-shaped coral are placed on some benches and in the plaid hammock that is slung diagonally across the end of the terrace.

PALM TREES

PALM TREES GROW NATURALLY IN
CORNWALL, BUT WE HAVE CREATED
SOME ARTIFICIAL ONES IN ORDER TO
INCREASE THE IMPRESSION OF FAR-
OFF SHORES. THE IMAGE OF A
FORMALIZED PALM WAS STENCILLED
IN SHARP FRESH GREENS AND
GOLDEN YELLOWS ON TO
HARDBOARD. PLACED TOP-TO-TAIL
ON A LARGE STANDARD-SIZED SHEET
MEASURING 2.4 x 1.2 M (8 x 4 FT),
WE FOUND WE COULD FIT IN TWO
TREES. A JIGSAW FITTED WITH A FINE
BLADE WAS USED TO CUT OUT
AROUND THE JAGGED SHAPE.

IF THERE IS NOT TIME TO GO TO
THE TROUBLE OF MAKING A STENCIL
FOR THE PALMS, IT WOULD BE EASY
TO DRAW DIRECTLY ON TO THE
HARDBOARD AND CUT AROUND THE
DRAWN IMAGE. HOWEVER, IF YOU
WOULD LIKE A FAIR NUMBER OF
TREES TO CREATE A MORE POWERFUL
EFFECT, IT IS WELL WORTH GOING TO
THE TROUBLE OF CUTTING A STENCIL
AS IT IS SO EASY TO REPEAT.

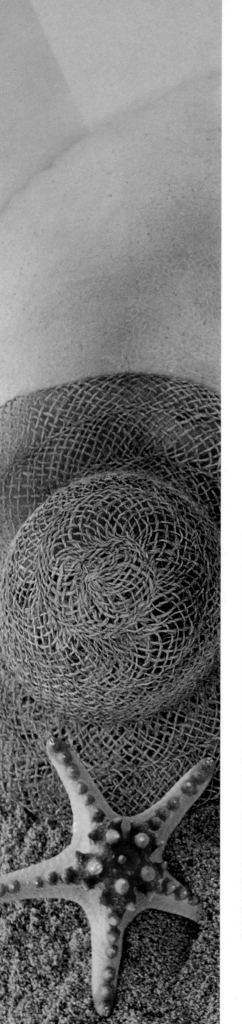

Dishes of fish and fruit are laid out on the table. The fruit is in crudely carved wooden bowls like Gauguin's; the fish is presented on plain white plates that have a garland of shells stuck around their rims. A large green-rimmed clear plastic bowl contains the punch and the disposable plastic 'glasses' have been sprayed with a similar blue-green paint.

SARONGS

Anemones are flowers that grow early in Cornwall because of our favourable Gulf Stream, but although colourful, they never grow in these hues, which have more in common with the palette of Gauguin. My huge stencil of anemones is brought out to imprint some lengths of plain cotton cloth to create special sarongs for our party. A sarong makes an easy cover-up after a swim or for paddling in the first waves, and if spread out on the sand, you can lie on it.

With such a large area of cut stencil, the work

of stencilling a length of cloth 182 x 122 cm (70 x 48 in) doesn't take long. However, a smaller stencil of a single flower could do the job; it just takes longer to cover the ground. There is precious little making-up involved - just a narrow hem around the edges. Then the sarong is ready to wrap around the body, secured by tucking the corner into the front.

We have printed off the same design in different colourways: one is in soft greens and the other, more colourful one is in mellow oranges and blues.

BEACH PARAPHERNALIA

There are few adults who do not succumb to the childlike pleasure of a dancing kite and, in its classic form, a kite is so easy to make.

We sprayed some sheets of thin paper (newsprint) with random speckles of yellow, blue and coral pink paint, letting the colours gently overlap. A simple framework was made of thin cane tied together with cotton thread. The longer cane in the cross shape measured 50 cm (20 in), the shorter one 25 cm (10 in). Paper was then stretched across the structure and glued to the outer edge canes framing the classic cross.

A tail of string, three times the length of the kite and joined to its base, has paper bow ties attached at 10 cm (4 in) intervals. The kite's tethering string is joined to 25 cm (10 in) long strings coming from each corner of the kite. These corners also sport cut paper tassels.

The kite is a joyful sight darting about as it catches the last of the sun.

To guard against gusty changes in the weather I had a wind-shelter made from natural canvas. I striped it with bold broad divisions made with masking tape, then I overlaid this apricot striping with a large-scale stencil of an agapanthus at its base. I stencilled it in its own strong colours of olive green and a purplish blue. These impressive blooms flower wildly along the edges of beaches on the nearby Isles of Scilly, so they look at home on a wind-break.

After stencilling is complete, the edges and slots for poles can be machine stitched (canvas is too heavy for hand work). Broom handles can be

The large stencil with the anemone design is ready for printing off pattern on to the lengths of cotton for sarongs. Wearing their individual sarongs, two of the party stroll along the water's edge. The colouring of the stencilled cloth merges with the evening light (far left). The softly coloured paper kites are simple to construct and are more robust than they appear. They will even take a dipping (left).

CORAL CUSHIONS

THE MATT SURFACE OF RAW SILK IS PERFECT FOR TAKING THE DELICATE IMPRINT OF STENCILLING FROM A PIECE OF CORAL. I PICKED UP MANY OF THESE CORALS LYING DISCARDED BY THE TIDE, FLATLY EMBEDDED IN THE SMOOTH AND DAZZLING SAND IN FRONT OF MY BROTHER'S HOUSE IN THE CARIBBEAN – AN ALMOST DAILY HARVEST.

IT IS VERY EASY TO SPRAY WITH PAINT THROUGH THE WEBBED STRUCTURE OF THE CORAL ON TO THE READY-CUT CLOTH. THE CUSHIONS ARE STITCHED TOGETHER IN A FAN SHAPE, THEN UNCOVERED PIPING CORD IS SEWN DOWN EACH STRAIGHT SIDE AND KNOTTED AT THE BASE, WHERE IT IS THREADED WITH TWO CARVED CHINESE BEADS.

used as poles to be driven deeply into the sand to secure the whole contraption when it is windy.

A local weaver of beautiful and imaginative baskets conjured up our enormous picnic basket using a brief sketch and a scrap of cloth as design inspiration. The cane was dyed specially in this lovely multicoloured array of sunset tones.

The appeal of a beach party lies in its unstructured format, and a relaxed indecision sets in. Fly a kite before supper, help with the cooking or swim. Doze in the hammock or concoct a refreshing punch. Collect driftwood for the fire or to construct a rustic seat to watch the setting sun. It is merely the degree of light that directs the action and eventually torches will be needed to collect the bits and pieces from amongst the rocks and sand before returning home. Then the next tide will sweep the whole beach clean.

BEACH TOWEL
A PLAIN WHITE TOWEL IS STENCILLED ACROSS AT RANDOM WITH SEA-GREEN PAINT, USING AN ORIGINAL OLD-FASHIONED METAL STENCIL WHICH WAS GIVEN TO ME. THIS IMPRINTS IT WITH A STRANGE BUT SUITABLE LABEL: 'SCILLY ISLES POOL'.

The apricot wind-shelter protects the picnickers from beach gusts (left). It is decorated with a simple agapanthus stencil (above).

Autumn

HARVEST SUPPER

'ALL IS SAFELY GATHERED IN' AND THERE IS A LULL IN WHICH TO BE THANKFUL
FOR EARTH'S MIRACULOUS GIFTS, SPRUNG FROM MERE SEEDS IN THE RICH EARTH
TO SUCH A GLORIOUS FLOWERING. AT THIS TIME OF ABUNDANCE, IT IS AN EASY
PLEASURE TO PRODUCE A RUSTIC SUPPER.

Richly glazed treacle tart glows against blue-green herbs and vegetables (left).
Suspended rosy apples and a great moon of cheese enliven the
harvest table (above).

Inspiration

In preparation for this farmer's supper, the best deserved of all the year after the labour of the harvest, I gather together the most natural and harmonious of ingredients. The colours of the earth – all the ochres, the deepest of summer's sky blue and the most vivid, unfaded greens – make up my palette.

I cover the trestle tables in generous lengths of crudely printed sacking and add cheerful basic kitchen checks. Terracotta pots of all shapes and sizes are brought into use and display most of the abundant fare. Also there are simple wood fruit troughs from France. Dressed up with thick plaits of straw bound to their hooped handles and filled with an array of trimmed vegetables, they make wonderful offerings at the church for the Harvest Festival.

In autumn an orchard makes a fine display of its crop with apples, pears, plums or cherries emblazoned on every tree. Ripe apples coupled together with intricately woven straw dollies make apt decorations.

Dough made from the first milling of the new grain is fashioned and baked into breads of explicit harvest imagery. The whole homely process of preparation of this supper is an intrinsic part of the festival. Traditionally, when all farm hands were busy in the fields, the women joined in the labour to produce the feast. Across the country, in kitchens, sculleries and larders, the timeless actions of mixing, stirring, heating and preserving went on. A communal effort, using as its ingredients the fruits of the warming summer sun. The result was hospitality of the most fundamental kind.

HARVEST BREADS
GOLDEN GLAZED BREADS STAND AS
PROVEN TOKENS OF A SUCCESSFUL
HARVEST. MALLEABLE DOUGH IS
FORMED INTO A VARIETY OF
TRADITIONAL DESIGNS SUCH AS A
RESPLENDENT SHEAF OF CORN OR
THE BIBLICAL DISPLAY OF SEVEN
LOAVES AND FIVE FISHES LAID OUT
ON A BREAD PLATTER WITH A
BROADLY PLAITED RIM.

ANY CHILD WHO HAS HANDLED
PLASTICINE WILL DELIGHT IN JOINING
IN WITH KNEADING, ROLLING AND
SHAPING THE SPRINGY DOUGH,
FASHIONING IT INTO STALKS AND
GRAINS AND EVEN A LONG-TAILED
HARVEST MOUSE. THE DOUGH IS THE
STANDARD MIX AND THE GLAZE IS
BEATEN EGG YOLK, CAREFULLY
BRUSHED OVER THE COMPLICATED
SURFACES.

I have talked about harvesting in its most commonly perceived form, that of bringing in the grain for our basic diet. The process and all the words associated with it are time-worn and familiar. The very sound of words like 'gathering' and 'gleaning', 'swaths' and 'scythes' have soothing connotations. In reality the process could be heartbreaking as well as backbreaking. But, like birth itself, nature's anaesthetic tends to leave us with only the pleasurable recollections.

Wherever man toils to produce sustenance, the pleasure of the reaping is turned into a ritual and celebrated. I recall here a handful of these seemingly perpetual events. The great grape harvests which swoop around the world, following closely the warmed path of the sun; the shearing of vast lands that produce hundreds of miles of the world's grains; or the more watery harvest of fish from the oceans. These are the grand harvests and the many people involved with these operations have the best of reasons to make merry as they pull in the last load.

There is, however, a totally different, more personal kind of harvest which one can just as validly feel proud of achieving. It may only be preserving and pickling the produce from the garden or the local market, or concocting some hedgerow brews of elderflowers or elderberries. It could be some timely plucking of hops, or even just filling jam jars with blackberries to cook with apples for pies. From the grand to the humble, the scale is of no consequence. Just set up a supper and celebrate.

Ensuring an adequate supply of the daily bread has always been and still is man's most primitive drive, although these days it is disguised in many an artificial cloak. It is no wonder that in rural communities the process of gathering the harvest safely in from the fields is drenched with ritualized customs. These are mostly expressions of pleasurable relief. In the past every man, woman and child would be called upon to ensure a swift and successful 'Harvest Home'. The success, or otherwise, spelt out the comparative prosperity or hardship for not only the farmer, but for the whole neighbourhood, for the year that followed.

While the women worked across the field, wielding their sickles to ground, slashing down

This graceful lantern-shaped dolly (left) fashioned from the last stand of corn in the field is symbolically hung by a farmhouse fireplace. It is thought to be sheltering the spirit of the corn in safety through the winter months. Yellow heads of corn have their stalks tightly manoeuvred into rhythmical forms (above). These plaited circles of dough perform a dual purpose, napkin rings and then as delicious supper rolls (below).

line after line of standing corn in waves, the men followed in formation, dealing with the fallen corn, systematically forming it into sheaves and then subsequently into stocks. These then formed bands across the stubbly fields, where they stood in the sun for a few days of final ripening before all was hauled back into the rickyards for winter storage. Finally the children combed the fields to the very edges for any gleanings that had fallen by the wayside. The field was then well shorn, apart from one last stand, left in the middle.

In this area of farmsteads, where the small fields are surrounded by 'hedges' of granite boulders which have been cleared from the earth, there still survives a custom called 'The crying of the neck'. It involves the ceremonious cutting of the last stand of corn, which is thought to contain the 'spirit of the harvest'.

Gathered around this last swath in the centre of the field the harvesters quench their thirst with cider. Then a cry will ring out three times, 'We have it!', followed by 'What have you?', which is answered by 'A neck! A neck! A neck!'. This haunting cry will carry for miles. In times gone by it was not uncommon on a particularly fine summer's evening to hear this call from many directions, as harvest after harvest was jubilantly brought to a close.

When cut, this handclasp of corn, the so-called 'neck', is tied about with field flowers and leaves and exultantly taken back to the farmer's house, accompanied by the exuberant workers. Here this trophy of the harvest is hung above the kitchen hearth. It sometimes stayed there only till Christmas Day, at which point it was taken out in the morning and fed to the cow of the herd that yielded the most milk.

The procedures surrounding the honouring of this last clasp of corn are ancient and varied. Similar talismans can be traced to the earliest roots of countries throughout the world; however, within each country, the exact procedure adopted varies from region to region. This suggests that it is the basic principle behind each of these rituals that is deeply embedded in the most primitive part of man's nature. In some areas, the honour accorded to the corn dolly evolved around the belief that the corn spirit nested in it

during the winter months, having fled into the centre of the field when the corn was being cut. During the spring sowing, it was returned to the fields where it could retreat into the corn, transferring its power to the new seed.

More ritual is associated with the rick building that followed the field work. Apparently it was such an honour to pitch the first sheaf on to the

A bread corn sheaf, as formal as a pub sign, is a great sight as it is pulled from the oven, complete with tiny glistening harvest mouse.

MAKING A LANTERN

THESE RUSTIC LANTERNS ARE MADE OUT OF OLD PAINT TINS. A PIECE OF BROWN PAPER MARKED OUT WITH PATTERN IS SECURED AROUND THE TIN WITH MASKING TAPE. THE TIN IS THEN FILLED WITH SAND TO GIVE IT BODY, AS THE SURFACE IS PIERCED BY HAMMERING A NAIL THROUGH THE METAL AT THE POINTS MARKED OUT ON THE DESIGN. A CONE OF FAN-SHAPED METAL IS ALSO PIERCED AND ITS EDGE OF DECORATIVE SCALLOPS CUT ALONG WITH METAL SNIPS. A SMALL FLUTED DISC IS SECURED AT THE TOP TO PREVENT THE WARMTH FROM THE CANDLE RISING TO OVERHEAT THE STRAPPY TIN HANDLE.

rick that it was dubiously rewarded with a wine-glass full of neat gin. The topmost sheaf was called the 'crow' and on achieving this the whole company was allowed to imbibe. This recalls the scene from Thomas Hardy's *Far from the Madding Crowd*, in which his hero, Gabriel Oak, wrestled alone to save the uncovered rick from the ravages of a sudden storm, while all about him farm-hands lay in a helpless stupor. Here in Cornwall, out on the far tip of this windlashed peninsula, the hayricks were covered in fish netting with stones sewn into the edges to weight them down. The narrow trestles that stretch across the yard are clothed in crudely printed hessian sacking. Fun was had as grown-ups returned, with giggles, to the childish pursuit of potato cuts, cutting, painting and smudgily printing the rough sacking with wildly swooping festoons. Instead of pota-toes, large curving marrows are halved length-ways and the new flat surface cut away until only the form of a leafy branch remains. Also an avo-cado pear is halved and, by simply removing the large central stone, it is possible to print out its lovely fruity shape among the leaves. As an allu-sion to branded corn sacks, I use only black for this printing and, because the sacking will not be washed, a child's poster paint is fine as the colouring agent.

Placed at each end of the tables are some wooden fruit baskets. I saw them lined up in a shop window

Places are set at the supper table in the lee of an old barn. Over this table hangs a wheel-like ring of candles suspended from a pole poked through an upper loading bay (above). A baked apple, with its hollowed-out core stuffed with sultanas and raisins, brown sugar and cinnamon. Small brown paper carrier bags are lined with up to 2.5 cm (1 in) of dried sand. The sand holds the lighted candles which act as glowing markers for the paths to the party in the failing light (right).

in southern France filled with lusciously ripe plums. I have tied plaits of straw over the simple hooped handles, securing them down each side with a knotted strip of checked cotton. Filled with an array of herbs and vegetables, they would be fine for taking to the church Harvest Festival.

Before this time of settled land and systematic farming, men lived as hunter gatherers, wandering the country continuously in search of food. It was the processes of planting and harvesting that led to the growth of farming communities around particular fertile areas. It is still this sense of mutual support that holds our scattered rural villages together. Harvest suppers these days are not so much as they used to be, a feast supplied by a grateful farmer for all those who assisted with harvesting. They are more an occasion at which a whole neighbourhood gets together for a general gesture of thanksgiving. The romance of an old-

style harvest supper is difficult to resist and the planning of it comes as naturally as it ever did - for whatever country our ancestors hail from, they would be familiar with the Harvest spirit.

As autumn approaches, the sun-ripened produce is all about us, making the task of providing for many people sitting down together for supper an easy one. At its simplest the meal can consist of a ploughman's lunch with great rounds of mature cheese, fresh and crusty herb bread and home-made fruity pickles. However this may not be grand enough for a special day in the country. Various cuts of meat and roasted fowl are in order here. Accompanied by the choicest of vegetables, flavours will be heightened by eating outside on the last warm evening of the year.

I have prepared a dish of mackerel, packed in tightly, head-to-tail, with bay leaves, their glistening chevroned skins camouflaged against the mottled blue markings of the shallow bowl. Soused in wine vinegar and laced with finely cut onion rings, they are delicious cold.

The favourite pudding to be eaten in the Duchy of Cornwall on 'The Great Day' was Wheat-Stack pudding. Made in a proper china pudding basin, this rich fruity mix was wrapped in a scalded cloth and boiled for several hours. When the cloth was removed, a cupful of the cooked mixture was scooped away from the top and replaced with brown sugar and clotted cream. A treat indeed for the farming families.

Today I prefer to offer what I call the golden puddings: a shallow tart with an open lattice-work top over breaded treacle, a light and spongy bread-and-butter pudding with a crusty top, or spicy stuffed baked apples, glazed in their own sugary juices. Wicked golden-crusted clotted cream is offered to those who dare indulge.

The utensils I am using for the party are chosen for their robust and rustic nature, great earthenware jugs, bowls and dishes. I made a point of filling them with trimmed, but uncooked vegetables, simply for display. Old family dinner plates are taken down off the dresser and lined up along the tables on colourful, brand new kitchen cloths. These cloths form soft, individual place settings on the rougher hessian and make capacious napkins.

Placed beside each plate is a straw corn dolly which goes by the name of a 'Countryman's Favour'. This is because they were traditionally woven by young swains as they walked with their sweethearts after church. The finest, most supple straw was plucked for the weaving of these dollies. The word 'dolly' is derived from 'idol'.

As the supper party draws to a close, a vast golden disc rises over the darkening fields, the most spectacularly romantic harvest moon.

THE CORNUCOPIA
THE CORNUCOPIA, SYMBOL OF PLENTY, IS SUPPOSED TO HAVE BEEN CREATED BY THE GOD ZEUS. FILLING A RAM'S HORN FULL OF THE SEEDS OF EDIBLE PLANTS, HE PRESENTED IT, IN GRATITUDE, TO THE NYMPHS THAT CARED FOR HIM AS A BABE. IT WAS TO ENSURE A PERPETUAL SUPPLY OF FOOD FOR THEM. AS A CENTREPIECE TO OUR SUPPER TABLE, WHAT COULD BE MORE APT? ON A SKELETON OF WIRE, THE VOLUPTUOUS SHAPE OF THE HORN IS FORMED WITH PAPER AND COVERED WITH CUT STRIPS OF HESSIAN, GLUED ON WITH WALLPAPER PASTE. FILLED WITH A GENEROUS ARMFUL OF WHEAT, IT DOMINATES THE TABLE.

GOLDEN WEDDING

A QUIET LUNCH PARTY TO CELEBRATE A COUPLE'S GOLDEN WEDDING HAS BEEN FITTINGLY ARRANGED IN AN OLD WELL-SEASONED DINING ROOM. SWEET-SMELLING POSIES OF HERBS, THAT WILL, WHEN DRY, LAST FOREVER, ARE PLACED AROUND THE TABLE FOR EACH GUEST. THE FAMILY IS EXPECTED AND WILL GATHER AROUND TO TOAST THE COUPLE WITH CHAMPAGNE, FIFTY YEARS AFTER THEY WERE FIRST TOASTED AT A DIFFERENT CELEBRATION, THEIR WEDDING. IT IS AN EVENT TO ACKNOWLEDGE, AN ACHIEVEMENT OF THE BEST KIND, WHEN PROMISES MADE LONG AGO HAVE BEEN FULFILLED.

*The cool autumn light at the window is warmed by this mellow lunchtime
table. A sprawling vine is stencilled around the base of the tablecloth with blue
velvety grapes and dark pink and wine-coloured leaves.*

Inspiration

The whole theme of the Golden Wedding party is based on the vine, and, in particular, the vine in autumn with the harvesting symbolizing the rewards of good husbandry.

The inspiration for colour and texture is also drawn from the heart-warming richness of autumnal vineyards, ranging from the deepest group of wine, mulberry, burgundy and maroon, to cobalt blue and a mid green, and on to the bright sheens of copper and gold and the paleness of mushroom pink and ecru. These colours, in combination with the 'grown-up' textures of lace, velvet and chintz, provide an atmosphere of wonderful mellowness.

Huge woody branches of hawthorn berries lodged in a long wooden trug, dominate the table, stretching high and right down its length. This mass of berries is interspersed with wonderful wine-red velvet hydrangeas; their great flowering heads are so stunningly coloured, it is difficult to believe they are natural. Even the backs of the leaves are an extraordinary shade of soft burgundy. Coming from a neighbouring garden, they steal the show.

Flanking a screen are a pair of pink-coloured urns filled with these berries and hydrangeas and sweeping sprays of vine leaves. These urns, which started their life as stark white plastic, have been elevated by being generously sprayed with a special paint finish that produces a thick mottled texture; they are now transformed into passable elegance. The gleaming golden leafy screen acts as a flattering backdrop to the honoured pair as they sit together at the head of the table.

VINE LEAF LAMPSHADE

Having chosen the vine with all its decorative lucidity as the keynote to our party, we proceed to use it liberally when setting about making our special effects. Of all forms of plant decoration, the vine has probably been used the most prolifically. Its pliant branches intertwine on grand textiles, objet d'arts and battered wooden inn signs. Its curvaceous leaves are ideal for superimposing on to the lampshade. With the variety of leaf sizes we are able to pluck from the vines, we can instil a lively rhythm on the border, with the largest zig-zagging through the middle and the smallest gently breaking into the faded edges. Springy tendrils are simulated by winding string tightly around a pencil; after a while they can be released and placed among the leaves before spraying. This process reminds me of my grandmother untying the rags she had laboriously tied on to my unwilling hair to coax it into coiled ringlets.

MAKING THE LAMPSHADE
THIS SOPHISTICATED LAMPSHADE, ON WHICH THE LEAVES ARE CUT TO LET THROUGH CHINKS OF LIGHT, IS UNBELIEVABLY SIMPLE TO MAKE USING A STANDARD COTTON LAMPSHADE CLOTH. WE CURVE THE SHADE MATERIAL AROUND THE FRAME AND, HOLDING IT IN PLACE WITH MASKING TAPE, DRAW AROUND ITS PERIMETER. AFTER CUTTING OUT THE RESULTING TEMPLATE, WE LAY IT FLAT. NEXT WE PLACE SOME LEAVES IN A CURVE AROUND THE TEMPLATE, NOT TOO CLOSELY TO THE EDGES, AND SPRAY OVER THEM LIGHTLY WITH BRONZE PAINT. REMOVING THE LEAVES, WE PARTIALLY CUT AROUND THE SAME SIDE OF EACH LEAF PRINT WITH A CRAFT KNIFE. AFTER ASSEMBLING THE SHADE WITH FABRIC GLUE, WE GENTLY PUSH OUT THE CUT EDGES A LITTLE FROM THE MAIN SHAPE.

VINE SCREEN AND TABLECLOTH

I use the vine leaves again to create my edition of a Japanese screen. This is cut from marine plywood and each length is given a good coating of gold spray paint, creating a beautifully tactile surface.

I have already selected some handsome specimens of leaves from an overgrown vine and put them to be pressed between boards weighed down with heavy books. I then mask off a border 30 cm (12 in) wide and some 15 cm (6 in) in from the edge of the screen, which has now been assembled with full-length strips of piano hinges. Lying the whole screen flat, supported on a table, I space out the pressed leaves across its central panel. With a light coating of spray glue across their backs, they stay in their very precise positions. Outside the edge of the masked-off border I place leaves of approximately the same size quite close to each other all around the edge.

All the positioned leaves are sprayed over lightly with a deep bronze colour which tints each exposed part of the screen in a darker tone. Both the masking and the now-tinted leaves are gently pulled away from the screen, which is now strongly patterned with gold leaves and a plain gold border. Into this border I firmly press down rows of the biggest of these leaves, which are still very pliant from both their coatings of glue and paint, one on each side. They feel like tissue paper with a network of little thin ribs. A final coat of clear semi-matt polyurethane varnish protects the screen.

For the vine around the skirt of the tablecloth (pages 120 and 121), mulberry chintz was chosen for its rich warmth as a subtle back-up to the predominance of gold. Around this golden stencilled vine I plan to stick on some extra leaves. Using real leaves as a template, the shapes are cut out of suede cloth in two different tones of mulberry, one lighter and the other darker than the chintz. Added to the stencilled border, they boost its size and also create extra texture. The grapes are made from cobalt blue cloth, stuck in position with fabric glue.

The old dining room at Trereife has been witness to many a fine family party. My first memo-

DECORATED FIREPLACE
DRESSING UP A HOUSE FOR A
SPECIAL TIME OF CELEBRATION NEED
NOT BE CONFINED TO CHRISTMAS.
FOR THE GOLDEN WEDDING PARTY
WE FESTOON THE FIREPLACE, A
FOCAL POINT, PARTICULARLY ON A
CHILLY AFTERNOON. THE NARROW
MANTELPIECE OF THE SIXTEENTH-
CENTURY GRANITE SURROUND IS
JUST WIDE ENOUGH TO LODGE A
GREAT GARLAND OF GREEN HOPS,
SECURED IN THE CENTRE OF POSIES
OF HERBS. IN ELIZABETHAN TIMES
NOSEGAYS, AS THEY WERE CALLED,
WERE A NECESSARY PROTECTION
AGAINST THE FOUL AIR OF POOR
SANITATION. CLOVE-STUDDED
POMANDERS WERE ALSO USED FOR
THIS PURPOSE. HERE THERE IS ONLY
THE WOODSMOKE TO BLEND WITH.
MADE UP AS A TRADITIONAL
VICTORIAN POSY, THE DIVERSE
COLOURS OF THE HERBS AND
FLOWERS ARE GROUPED IN RINGS
AROUND A CENTRAL FLOWERHEAD.
GREY AND ACID GREEN HERB LEAVES
AND THISTLE HEADS DRIED A LOVELY
MAUVE ARE GROUPED AROUND A
LARGE PAPERY CRIMSON
HELICHRYSUM. SITTING IN A FRAME
OF BRONZE-SPRAYED PAPER LACE,
THEY LOOK QUITE PRECIOUS.

ries of it conjure up the huge mahogany table ringed with the faces of four generations, laughing and talking in the candlelight. Any excuse would do for a get-together that everyone from the oldest to the newest and the youngest would thoroughly enjoy. The meal would be followed by uproarious charades and other games, at which some particular talent of acting or wit would shine out for the first time among the youngsters as they gained their ground.

Above the mantelpiece in the dining room is a portrait of Charles Valentine Le Grice, a forebear, who was a minor Romantic poet of his time. Close companions of school-days at Christ's Hospital, and afterwards at Cambridge, were the illustrious literary figures of Coleridge, Lamb and Wordsworth. Later Coleridge was to say of him, 'Le Grice has buried himself away in Cornwall'. Here he surrendered to the pleasures of this delightful manor house and a certain rich young widow. For, coming down from Cambridge to tutor her son, he had subsequently married her and had a son of his own. When her own son died as a young man, the charmingly named Day Perry Le Grice became the successor to the estate.

Once again the dining room is decorated for a special lunch party, a Golden Wedding celebration. The fireplace is decked out with hops specially sent from Kent, the Garden of England. The dark furniture is given an extra polish so that it will truly gleam in the firelight. There is positive pleasure to be achieved from being indoors with a fire when all outside is misty and grey; a real antidote to the dullest autumn days. Add to this the reassuring gathering together of old friends and what other occasion could be nicer to anticipate?

Beige lace mats are placed as settings on the rosy chintz of the tablecloth, the kind that most grannies can dig out from the back of a drawer. They can come out into the light of day for this pastiche of an old-world setting. Beside each mat is placed one of the sweet-smelling posies of herbs, given as keepsakes to take home.

Little custard pots of crème caramel, with golden pears on the lids, are placed on showy golden dishes with small silver spoons with deli-

cate handles like twisted twigs. This is the pudding. However, the lunch party starts with a soup made with Jerusalem artichokes, followed by flamboyantly dressed pheasant, with an array of pared-down autumn vegetables arranged on a wonderfully large platter.

A deep ripe Stilton topped up with port is to be scooped out and eaten with Bath Oliver biscuits. The famous Doctor Oliver of Bath, who concocted this classic recipe, originally came from near Penzance, from the outlying village of Gulval. There are baskets of apples for those who want fruit; these small friendly russets, with the mellow texture of tarnished gold, are the epitome of autumn to me. Finest Java coffee is poured to sip during a few informal speeches, while glistening crystallized fruit from the South of France is passed around.

The choice of a lunchtime rather than an evening party seemed the most suitable as it leaves the remainder of the day for talks around the fire, going over old times while a few chestnuts are roasting. Then plenty of time is left to return before night sets in.

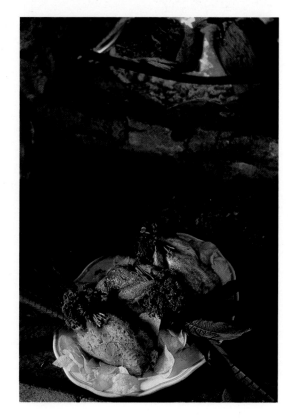

LEAF MIRROR FRAME
A PAPER BAG FULL OF GLOSSY GREEN CAMELLIA LEAVES, A MUG FULL OF BERRIES AND SOME ALL-PURPOSE GLUE ARE ALL YOU NEED FOR THE MIRROR. STICK DOWN THE LEAVES, OVERLAPPING LIKE A PLAIT, AND SPRINKLE ON A FEW BERRIES OVER A BLOB OF GLUE AT THE BASE OF EACH LEAF. LET THE GLUE DRY AS YOU WORK. IT'S A GOOD IDEA TO START CENTRALLY AT THE TOP OF THE FRAME, SO YOU CAN CHANGE THE DIRECTION OF THE FLOW AT THE CENTRE TOP AND CENTRE BOTTOM. THE LEAVES WILL DRY AND LOSE THEIR STRONG GREEN IN TIME, BUT A SWIFT SWEEP DOWN THE MIDDLE OF THE FRAME WITH COPPER METALLIC SPRAY PAINT HIGHLIGHTS THE BERRIES AND SOME LEAVES. HANG THE MIRROR IN PLACE TO DRY OUT THOROUGHLY.

ANNIVERSARY PRESENTS

Anniversary presents are always welcomed if they are personal gifts, however small. Remember that it is preferable to give a gift relevant to both parties. Home-made wrappings also show you care, the kind that granny would fold up and keep to show her friends. Plain sheets of tissue paper and sleek satin ribbons can be transformed. With a clutch of leaves and a few left-over cans of spray paint, blank sheets of black and white tissue paper are swiftly worked over. With a leaf in one hand and a can in the other, the leaf acts as a moving template, with puffs of paint registering each movement. With a change of colour the pattern becomes richer and denser; remember, however, that a limited colour range is smartest. This use of the leaf shape reminds me of early American theorem paintings on velvet.

I pull out some beige and white satin ribbons from my ribbon basket and lay some smart cotton artificial flower heads along them. Lightly sprayed over with bronze paint, they look exclu-sive and special, good enough for any proud granny.

To associate lavender with old ladies is a cliché, but it has to be admitted that most love it. How lovely if even grandpa's shirts could smell a little of lavender. These sachets can be put together by the smallest hands and paid for from the smallest purse. White lacy handkerchiefs have been allowed to soak in tea, strained from the pot. When dried and ironed, they are filled with loose lavender and securely tied up with narrow ribbons. A few drops of lavender essence adds to their potency. With their lacy corners pulled out and a stem of tiny cotton flowers pushed in, they make a pretty bundle.

FIRESCREEN

By the time most couples get to their Golden Wedding, they have reached that comfortable time when basic needs are well looked after. It is the personal extras, objects that have individual appeal tailored to their interest, that will give the

DÉCOUPAGE WASTE-PAPER BIN
MONOCHROME DÉCOUPAGE
DECORATES THIS TIN WASTE-PAPER
BIN. PREVIOUSLY SPORTING A
HIDEOUS DECORATION THAT WOULD
TAKE SOME LIVING WITH, IT HAS
UNDERGONE A GENTLE
RESTORATION. OVER A COVERING
SHEET OF BROWN PAPER, AN EARLY
ENGRAVING OF A HERO FROM
HAITIAN HISTORY HAS BEEN
METICULOUSLY CUT OUT AND GLUED
DOWN. SMALL OAK LEAVES HAVE
BEEN GLUED ON SEPARATELY TO FILL
ANY EMPTY SPACES AND A CLASSICAL
HERO'S BORDER OF LAUREL LEAVES IS
GLUED AS BINDING TO ITS BASE AND
RIM. A THICK LAYER OF VARNISH,
APPLIED IN SEVERAL COATS, GLOSSES
OVER THE SURFACE. THIS OBJECT,
WHICH STARTED LIFE SO
UNPROMISINGLY, CAN NOW TAKE ITS
PLACE IN A VENERABLE HOUSEHOLD.

greatest pleasure. Older people spend a great deal of their time sitting, talking and thinking about their offspring, when their routine tasks are done. This is fine when there is a lively fire to focus on, but in the summer months a fireplace can be a sad sight. An elegant firescreen cut into three Gothic-shaped panels could give a lot of pleasure, particularly if it displays images of much-loved members of a family.

Our screen is styled in the manner of an early Victorian print room. These rooms, worked on by inventive young ladies who pasted the walls with prints with elaborately cut-out paper frames on drawn-out winter afternoons, came under the category of 'pleasurable pursuits', and so they are. A brother and sister could work together to make a firescreen, and instead of the old-fashioned pictures, substitute photocopied photographs of their family. In fact, a whole family tree could be worked out on these panels.

To begin with we covered the panels, which were cut from 12 mm (^{1}/$_2$ in) plywood to measure 71 cm (28 in) high and 25 cm (10 in) wide, in plain brown wrapping paper. The quality of this

paper is so often overlooked, but with its faint stripe and honey brown colour it really is very distinguished. Years ago I papered a tiled hall with it, and it hit just the right note, causing many admiring comments. Here it provides just the required background texture on which to stick our images. Photocopies of bows and strips of decorative borders from magazines can be pasted around the images. Given a coat of varnish, which leaves it looking like a glossy chestnut, the screen is hinged together and finished off with a braid fixed on with brass-headed tacks.

Sheets of black tissue paper have been upgraded with an all-over leaf pattern sprayed across them. Lavender is bundled into lacy handkerchief sachets and trimmed with ribbons and cotton flowers (left). This elegant Gothic firescreen has been decorated in the manner of an old-fashioned print room with framed cut-out images (above).

Autumn

HOUSEWARMING

IN SOME PARTS OF EUROPE A TREE IS HAULED TO THE CHIMNEY TOP WHEN A HOUSE REACHES COMPLETION. THEN A PARTY IS GIVEN FOR ALL WHO CONTRIBUTED TO ITS SUCCESSFUL CONCLUSION, FROM THE ARCHITECT TO THE PLUMBER. IN ENGLAND AND AMERICA THERE WAS A CUSTOM OF BARN RAISING, WHEN NEIGHBOURING FARMERS GAVE A HAND LITERALLY TO RAISE THE BUILDING'S SUPPORTING TIMBERS. THEN A BOISTEROUS EVENING OF BARN DANCING FOLLOWED, A TRADITIONAL SHINDIG.

The hospitable glow radiating from the supper table and the window candles is enough to warm both home and heart. The gift of a painted wooden owl whose gentle movements will, it is hoped, instil a spirit of peace in its new home.

To set the party aglow I chose a room with golden yellow varnished walls, golden yellow glazed pottery and baskets of golden yellow chrysanthemums. Preparing the food is kept simple. Flour can be sieved and pancakes whisked up by guests willing to help with the cooking and they can choose their own fillings. There are plenty of lemons and a jug of maple syrup, or there is cheese and a bowl of fine shining black olives. Three different kinds of fruit loaves - a local yellow saffron loaf, a ginger brown malt loaf and a very white yeast bread - make a stripy display on the square platter. A large round basket offers seed and grain rolls while the small round basket of medlars is there just because someone brought it and it looks so lovely. The crunchy texture of the pecan pie has just the right rough-and-ready look for this party table.

The rooms of the house, all but bare except for essential furniture and some half-unpacked Indian tea chests, do not immediately present a party atmosphere. Flattering low lights will help. Unpack some lamps and pull out a few large storage jars. Without their glass tops and with ordinary household candles stuck into them, they impart something of the allure of hurricane lamps.

Other elements that at once add life and luxury to a room are plants and flowers. Guests may well come with plenty, but I bring armfuls of old-fashioned chrysanthemums from the garden, saved from the rising winds of the equinox. There is always a wonderful 'gala' feeling about a mass of flowers. A huge, fragile, gauzy network of dried-out twigs looks magical when lit from below by a lamp. The mellow atmosphere is now radiating a warmth as tangible as the hospitality.

With a spark of ingenuity in partnership with scissors, glue and paint, much can be done to give the impression of established, furnished comfort. The very wrappings and cartons you are about to dispose of as you unpack can be brought into further use for a dying moment of glory.

To eliminate the blankness of uncurtained windows I effected a pair of jokey pantomime curtains. Using large pieces of brown parcel paper, I stencilled a rather grand all-over design across its faintly lined, matt surface. Cut into

exaggeratedly curved shapes, I fixed them up around the frame of the window. These makeshift curtains look so good that they may well stay up longer than they should.

Taking advantage of all the corrugated cardboard lying around from unpacking, we cut up its deeply rutted surface into diverse shapes. Rearranged in layers with these ridges set at differing angles, it looks very effective. An extravagant façade is assembled from curly cut-out serpentine shapes stuck on to a cardboard apron to front the plain kitchen table. Even the mantelpiece is dressed with a zig-zagged geometric valance, which gives it a slightly Gothic look. Butted up flat to the top edge of the shelf, it is attached with double-sided adhesive tape. This stylish but ephemeral cladding is achieved at very little expense.

When we at one time changed a barn into our family home, we displaced a barn owl from its long-time residence. Its sad nightly circling of the building continued long after we were established in it, and it haunts me still. So the beautiful pale wooden owl brought into this house is bringing a presence that will stay, the friendliest of ghosts.

It is this kind of personal present that really contributes to the formation of a household. Lovely hand-marbled books for visitors and household records, and piles of towels complete with batons of lavender are also welcome. As would be the picturesque witch's broomstick with its spreading green bristles and its pair, an elegant, but equally useful cane carpet beater. It is, however, images like the rustic cockerel ready to rule over the kitchen, or the quirky amber-coloured wooden shoes to hang from a satin ribbon by the wardrobe, that strongly contribute to the particular personality of a house.

A jumble of housewarming presents, functional and decorative, clutters the decorated mantelshelf and a symbolic gift of kindling is placed next to the fireplace.

Winter

CHRISTMAS

IT IS SAID THAT CHRISTMAS IS FOR CHILDREN. HOWEVER, WE ALL HAVE A NEED FOR ITS WARMING SPIRIT OF FUN AND FESTIVITIES DURING THE LONG DARK DAYS OF WINTER. THE RELIGIOUS RITUALS, THE CANDLES AND COMMUNION OF MIDNIGHT MASS, THE FAMILY GATHERINGS AND THE ROUND OF PARTIES ALL ADD CHEER TO SEE US THROUGH THE COLD DEMANDING MONTHS.

The town's Silver Band visits the houses of Penzance to play carols (left). A peg angel in her regalia of golden sprayed lace and felt, and oranges and glistening evergreen leaves make wonderful festive decorations (above).

Inspiration

Christmas is a time when everything can be literally tipped with gold without fear of vulgarity. It is to remind us of the sun which, through these wintry days, if it appears at all, is a pale reflection of its summer glory. We can unashamedly seek out the gleam of metals, the glow of oranges, the red of embers and the gloss of deep dark greenery. Outside, the landscape is grey and brown and black, and the sea a chilling icy blue. We illuminate the rooms of our houses with parchment-shaded lamps, fairy lights, tree lights and the flickering light from fires and candles, and we hang lanterns at our doors. We draw richly textured fabrics across the blankness of our dark windows and for extra warmth and comfort as coverings for our beds. We concoct rich and filling dishes: plum pudding, mince pies, brandy butter and Christmas cake, stuffings and sauces, bonbons and crystallized fruits. We store up treats and delicacies, hide away secret presents and send our cards, invitations and gifts, to those far away, making contact for the first time in the year. We bring in logs and leaves, trees and nuts to add to this whole accumulated feeling of well-being. We festoon the house with evergreens, winding them down the stairway and around the rooms, over pictures, mirrors and mantelpieces, punctuated with groups of oranges, apples and fir cones, pineapples and nuts. In the hall we hang a kissing bough, enclosing mistletoe. The tree is strung with stars and bells and angels, and from the door knocker hangs a full wreath of greenery. On Christmas Day there will be bells in the air.

MAKING DECORATIVE BOXES

A wreath of ivy and mistletoe has been stencilled over the kitchen windows with snow spray to add cheer to the Christmas chores. Stored on the paper-trimmed shelves are some extra Christmas treats. I have always found it difficult to throw away unusually shaped boxes. Given new covers, linings and trimmings, they come to life again, making attractive and personalized containers for home-made sweets and biscuits.

Having sprayed a pattern from lace over some broad satinized paper bakery ribbons, I line both the inside and outside of some of the boxes. If the surfaces are too broad, I use paper that has been patterned similarly. The faithful doily now takes centre stage. Instantly transformed with a spray of gold and bronze paints, it is dissected into lengths of lacy trimming, individual flowers, scrolls and other elements. Stuck imaginatively in and around the containers they complete a look of luxury.

WRAPPING PAPER AND RIBBONS

I decide to set to and make some appealing material to wrap up the presents. Working over spruce new sheets of brown parcel paper, the kind with the elegant, faintly marked stripes, I transform their appearance with delicate, dense patterning. This is done by placing strips of synthetic lace closely together across the surface of the paper and spraying over them with gold and muted coloured paints.

Absurdly luxurious-looking ribbons are created in a similar manner. Paper straw ribbons are made in mouth-watering colours, but their usual use is inadvisedly to embellish mixed bouquets of flowers concocted by florists. My feeling is that they deaden the colours of the flowers and fight with their natural glory; for my part I can't take them off quickly enough. However, their satiny finish, when taken out of context and given some special extra texturing, has a different appeal, resulting in some grand-looking parcels.

THE CHRISTMAS TREE

Our tree at The Stencilled House – a fine, upstanding Nordic fir – stands in the hall, reaching to the first floor. Adorned in a gaudy theme of scarlet and gold, it is hung with bells, stars and the proverbial multitude of angels. These delightful angels (illustrated on page 135) are individually dressed up in splendidly regal costumes, cladding the simple form of a wooden clothes peg. Red felt, stencilled grandly in gold paint, forms the basis of their gowns and this is imaginatively trimmed with golden-sprayed lace in a great diversity of styles. Golden stars and wings are cut from cardboard. Frostings of gold glitter and gold sequins are glued on to the dressed image to add a finish of elaborate richness. Hung

from thin cottons, the guardians of the tree swirl around catching the light.

The old habit of going from house to house singing carols is still luckily very much alive in Cornwall and the Cornish are as proud of their choirs as their fellow Celts, the Welsh. It is the same with the silver bands; most of the small towns have one and they make the rounds at Christmas, adding greatly to the build-up of festivities. They stand in a group at doorways or, if the house will take them, enter and play grouped around the tree. To hear the sound of them singing around our old house is a particular pleasure each year and one that I know I will never tire of at all.

Sumptuous wrapping papers are easily made by spreading discarded curtain nets over plain newsprint paper and spraying on gold paint. Prettily shaped old boxes are revamped with satin ribbons and paper lace. Packed with home-made confectionery, they make thoughtful gifts, adding glamour to the Christmas supper table (left). The elaborately rich look of these wrapping papers and ribbons belies their cheap and simple beginnings of brown paper, bakery ribbons and synthetic lace (above).

THE PRESENTS

Crammed with wrapped presents and Christmas extras, this gilded cupboard conveys a strong message of the excitements in store. All kind of nuts, small fir cones and dried leaves have been elevated into beautiful trimmings by merely being dusted across with gold spray paint. This magical substance once again performs its fairy godmother act to great effect. Time is all that is needed now to create imaginative and tempting parcels.

One large box has each of its six surfaces chequered with satiny ribbons weaving in and out. Another parcel is wrapped in gold paper with an all-over stencilled design of flowers in a duller gold paint, giving it a texture like damask.

Thick, round candles and squat, square ones are delicately figured with lacy markings across their richly coloured wax surfaces. These gold paint marks will harmlessly disappear as the candle burns down. Bundles of ivory candles are tied together with sprays of gilded eucalyptus leaves and a filigree ribbon.

Pomanders have been with us since Elizabethan times and, in all likelihood, before. Sweet-smelling oranges stuck densely with cloves look more like crown jewels when every clove head is tipped with a thin spray of gold paint.

A parcel wrapped in woven florist's ribbons is simply stencilled with stars and moons in individual squares (above).

CHRISTMAS CRACKERS
YOUR CHRISTMAS TABLE CAN SPORT
THE MOST LAVISH AND
EXTRAVAGANT-LOOKING CRACKERS
IF YOU SPEND TIME MAKING YOUR
OWN. A CYLINDER, 28CM (11IN) IN
LENGTH, IS CUT INTO THREE
SECTIONS: 6CM (2IN) AT EACH END,
LEAVING 16CM (6IN) IN THE MIDDLE.
COVERING THESE WITH WHITE CREPE
PAPER, WE HAVE A FRILLY COLLAR AT
EACH END OF THE CRACKER. WE SLIP
A PAPER CRACKER TAPER THROUGH
THE MIDDLE AND INSERT A SMALL
GIFT, ACCOMPANIED BY A SUITABLY
PERSONALIZED LIMERICK AND A
TIGHTLY ROLLED-UP CREPE PAPER
PARTY HAT. THE OUTER COVERING
OF CREPE PAPER IS GENTLY PULLED
TOGETHER BETWEEN THE CUT
CYLINDERS OF CARD IN ORDER TO
SECURE THESE TRINKETS IN THE
CENTRE PORTION OF THE CRACKER.
IT IS THEN SECURED WITH A RING OF
ELASTICATED GOLD THREAD. WE
STICK ON LITTLE PLEATED GOLD FANS
AND PAPER IVY LEAVES, FOLDED
ALONG THEIR VEINING, WHICH ARE
CENTRED AROUND GROUPS OF
GILDED HAZEL NUTS.

CHILDREN'S DECORATIONS

It is fun for children to make their own decorations for their rooms and this can absorb them happily while everyone is busy doing something towards the preparations for the Christmas holiday. In order to make the paper chains, we have cut up some strips of lace-sprayed brown wrapping paper, measuring approximately 20cm (8in) long by 5cm (2in) wide. We use pinking shears to do this, so that the edges of each paper link are prettily serrated. The first ring is formed and the 1.3cm (1/2in) overlap secured with a brushful of flour-and-water paste. Through this ring is threaded the next strip, which is also glued together, and so it goes on. In no time a satisfying mound of chain is building up – nearly enough to loop gracefully around the nursery.

Paper lanterns are made to hang over the central light with the festoons of paper chains. These are made from sheets of stencilled parcel paper approximately 25cm (10in) deep and 38cm (15in) wide. With the paper folded in half lengthwise, the slashes are made by cutting in from the folded edge to a depth of 10cm (4in) at 2.5cm (1in) intervals. Opened up, the paper is glued together to form a cylinder and reinforced with collars at top and bottom to which hanging

The nursery of The Stencilled House hung with chains and lanterns. A special tea with gingerbread people is set ready for the workers (above). As day breaks in the nursery, it is clear that sabots have been filled. Fruit, nuts, sweets and little round biscuits are surrounded by toys (left).

straps are attached. The edges are punched with holes and a paper tassel is fixed to the underside like on a Chinese lantern.

The last oddments of paper are used to conjure up some papery peg angels for the mantelpiece. The feathery wings are made from serrated off-cuts from the trimmed edges of the paper chains.

TOYS AND TRADITIONS

I suppose it will always be the Victorian image of Christmas that is uppermost in our minds when we make our plans. In small ways we all want something of a 'real' Christmas: special china that only sees the light of day when Christmas is in the offing; the dinner table flanked by smaller ones in order to seat the descending family, and covered with a huge Christmas cloth; the excuse for candles everywhere without being labelled a 'Romantic'; the debate about the size and position of the tree and what goes on it.

Most important of all is the procedure around the hanging of the stockings, or the placing of the wooden sabots before the fire. The magical appearance of toys at Christmas makes it the most memorable time to receive them, and many childhood favourites were first glimpsed in the dawn light of Christmas morning. I like to make it as close to a scene from a story-book as I can. Here, in The Stencilled House, we set them around the nursery fireplace. Hidden amongst the fruits and other goodies are colourful and beautifully crafted knick-knacks from all over the world: a Chinese puzzle and a woven banjo-shaped pencil case filled with bright pencils; wooden tree toys from Czechoslovakia; a miniature box of dolls and an elaborate straw rattle from Mexico; and a pair of beautiful tall dolls made by American Indians. With the Russian horses that hang on the tree, the American popcorn and gingerbread from Holland, these items make up a meaningfully international Christmas, representing a broader family.

Making toys as presents or, indeed, revamping old ones, is the greatest fun. From an ambitious project like a doll's house or a horse and cart, to trains, planes, swings or simply bricks, engaging objects can be conjured up with off-cuts of wood,

pots of paint, glue, string, time and ingenuity. Refurbishing an old rocking horse, dressing a favourite doll or making new quilts and covers for a toy cot can give a great deal of pleasure to both the giver and receiver.

I remember the sheer, unbelieving joy of walking into a room at Christmas when I was a very young child and seeing before me a home-made doll's house made for me and my sister by an incredibly kindly neighbour, with all the windows lit up with torch bulbs, the batteries cleverly hidden in the roof. I also remember a beautifully painted toy rocking cradle that a German prisoner-of-war made for me. He worked on our farm and he had applied my name on to the rocking cradle, endearingly spelt wrong in a heart surrounded by delicately painted flowers – a treasure.

THE CHRISTMAS FEAST

The Christmas celebrations of old in Cornwall were lusty affairs. One such is described in an old book of Cornish houses and customs. It took place at the old manor house of Trewoofe at the head of the Lamorna valley. The women there were up before dawn on Christmas morning to start their baking and roasting for the feast. The men were up and out early, too, off into the valleys and hills to go hunting with their farming neighbours. The carrying call of their bugle-horn told those at home of their progress. The great fireplace at the hall was roaring with logs of sweet-smelling wood, with spits and pans set before it cooking all manner of meats and poultry.

All afternoon huntsmen returned in waves, hungry as hounds, to be fed at the Squire Lovell's table. This splendid table was laden with 'steaming bowls and tankards, piles of apples, roasted and raw, and heaps of sweetcakes', all set amid 'great burned candlesticks standing on the table'. The old house was hung with branches of holly, box and bay, with garlands of ivy at the windows. Tunes were beaten out on pewter and brass pots and pans to accompany tambourines in making music for dancing. The feasting and dancing continued into the night. It was dawn again before the party broke. With the draining of stirrup cups, the guests were seen off by the Squire with shouts of 'Merry Christmas to one and all!'

It all sounds extraordinarily exuberant and full-blooded if we compare it with our own attempts at celebrating Christmas. However, this kind of occasion really can still be relished if we spurn all editions of pre-packed fun. Set an extravagantly theatrical scene and people will enter into the spirit of it and live it out. It is not necessary to go out chasing the deer to appreciate a veritable feast; an ambitious Christmas walk would have the same effect.

A carved and gilded fish is lit mysteriously by night lights set in little terracotta pots (above). An elegant wall-mounted candelabra of painted wood is further ornamented with trailing ivy (middle). The darkly rich Christmas pudding is aflame with brandy. Ringed with holly, it takes centre stage after the turkey (below).

Set in the dining room of The Stencilled House, with its grape border ringing the room and hooping over the ceiling, we have continued with the theme of fruit and greenery. We tend to be so blasé about the beauty of the orange, but I have used these glowing orange spheres to punctuate the sheaves of evergreen that hang abundantly about the room. Their colour is so classically complementary to the glossy deep green leaves. Sparked off with touches of gold in the form of table ornaments, this rich colour combination is seen against the perfect foil of a white damask tablecloth.

A pair of reindeer face each other along the breadth of the table. They have baubles hanging from their antlers and trails of ivy spring from pots on their backs. Their finely carved wooden heads look splendid sprayed with my favourite gold paint. The turkey on the mantelpiece goes through a similar transformation.

The centrepiece of the table is set on a square of gold lace: a dark leafy bowl on a stand is piled high with layers of oranges, alternating with layers of golden spheres made of wire mesh. This gives the oranges an intriguingly suspended appearance. The same gold mesh makes pretty baskets, which are filled with sweetmeats and set beside each leaf green plate. At each end of the table are robust wooden candlesticks with quite large dishes at the top to catch the wax. I have glued into these dishes clusters of nuts and cones spiked with bay leaves. Once again gold spray paint transforms the whole arrangement into beautiful ornaments.

Shallow oval baskets made of twigs and leaves are filled with exotic gold nuggets; they are, in fact, brazil and other nuts that have had the gold spray treatment. They remain quite edible as their shells are cast away, and are unbelievably attractive.

When it was first imported from America, the turkey represented a dish of great luxury. It is now so extensively farmed that this is sadly no longer so. However, I think everyone would agree that it is the sauces and stuffing that make this dish special at Christmas. Sweet fruits, savoury roots and herbs are prepared in a timeworn manner, harking back to ancient feast days, to

make up the diversity of traditional tastes.

I like to make our Christmas pudding by boiling it suspended in a cotton cloth to keep its old-fashioned rounded shape, just as it is drawn in children's comics. During its mixing, everybody must stir it and make a wish – originally, perhaps, a ploy to engage many hands in the task. It is at this time that I slip in silver threepenny pieces to be boiled in the pudding, ready to clink on to lucky plates, gleaming amidst the dark fruit, as it is served aflame with brandy.

The table at the end of the Christmas feast. Sweetmeats in little golden woven baskets are set beside each place to be taken by guests as a memento. The mantelpiece is dominated by a huge straw turkey, resplendent in a sprayed-on coat of gold. Bedded in greenery, wooden oranges line up along a lower shelf and models of St Nicholas stand at each end.

NEW YEAR'S EVE MASKED BALL

THE PERIOD BETWEEN CHRISTMAS AND TWELFTH NIGHT HAS ALWAYS BEEN A TIME OF HIGH FESTIVITY AND CENTRAL TO THESE CELEBRATIONS IS NEW YEAR'S EVE. SEEING THE NEW YEAR IN USED TO BE A MOST UNINHIBITED AND JOYOUS OCCASION. IN THE STAGING OF THIS BALL, MY AIM IS TO URGE A RETURN TO MORE EXCITING AND GLAMOROUS EVENTS THAT LIFT US RIGHT OUT OF OUR WINTER LETHARGY TO GREET THE NEW YEAR WITH SOME GUSTO.

Party finery is laid out in readiness and fantastic masks are propped up against the stone mullions of a high window in the ballroom (left and above).

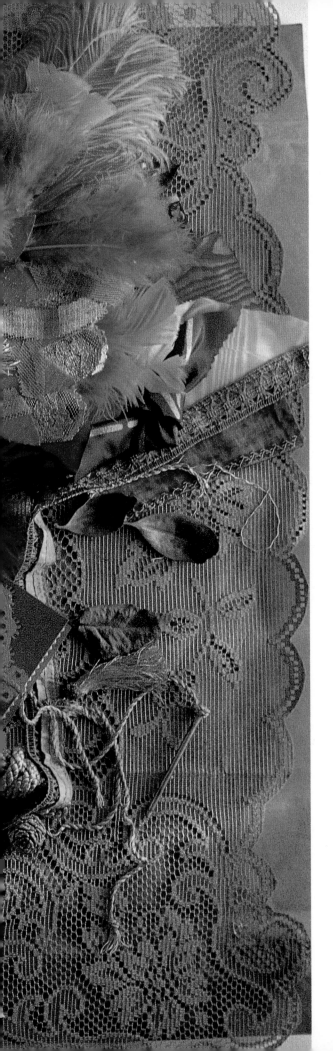

Inspiration

There is no need to quell my natural inclination towards the theatrical with the staging of this event. A Masked Ball must be imbued with a sense of drama as excitement runs high.

With beautiful Godolphin as our stage, a sixteenth-century country house, we have a setting as romantic as a scene on a tapestry, a woodland glade set about with ancient walls. Colours will be rich and luxurious, and textures elaborate with a feeling of antiquity. Imagine ivory parchment satin, hand-painted with exquisite finely stemmed flowers and insects, reminiscent of Elizabethan stumpwork embroidery, shot silks and watered taffeta or the yellowing of Spitalfield silk, with trailing gem-like flowers. Such cloths can be imitated with cheap substitutes and stitched up into some handsome costumes, billowing canopied dresses, deeply bodiced and ruffled at the elbows, or fine waistcoats and breeches. Gold of every hue from the faintest, palest tint of gilt to the richest, deepest, copper-bronze highlights many surfaces. Acting as a backing to these beautiful golds are a selection of gorgeous blues, turquoise, Prussian and peacock. In addition, that particular false green found inside china cupboards, specially painted there to enhance the richly patterned contents. Warmer tones are represented by mulberry, salmon and shocking pinks and a startling cerise.

The treasure chest of exotic masks lies open to one side of the wicket gate leading to the courtyard at Godolphin. Guests may equip themselves with a mask if they have come without. A pair of harlequin figures in the shape of dummy boards flanks the entrance in attendance. The robust spikes of silver-grey yucca plants are plainly set in steely buckets along the colonnade and the pathways are marked out with lines of candle lanterns.

We set out to create masks so exotically bizarre that the rest of the costume is merely a foil. The cut-out shapes of the cardboard masks are covered in richly embellished cloths and mounted on pea-sticks, entwined with ribbons. Much use of braids and laces helps to build up elaborate textures. Among the disparate bits and pieces gathered to decorate the masks are brilliant blue feathers plucked from a feather duster, sequined fishes, bunches of glossy cherries, dried flowers, gold tinsel, sequins and all manner of ribbons, cords, tassels and nets.

THE SETTING

We are extremely fortunate in being able to use a nearby sixteenth-century house, Godolphin, to stage our ball. Standing through the centuries in its placid woodland setting, the gaunt beauty of its colonnaded façade is breathtaking. The fine granite house was built up from the wealth accrued when the Godolphins were the leading mining family of the county, in Tudor times.

There is hardly a region that does not have its own scattering of beautiful houses and sometimes it is possible that the owners may be generous and amenable about making their houses available for similar events, particularly if any proceeds are donated to some pertinent benefit.

HARLEQUINS

In the early 1800s, the revelry of the guise dancers in the streets of Penzance reached such a pitch at New Year that the atmosphere was compared to an 'Italian Carnival'. It will always be Venice that springs to mind at the mention of carnivals. There, elegantly cloaked and masked crowds gather in those spacious piazzas and prominent among them are the dashing harlequins of the *commedia dell'arte* in their diamond-cut colours. The blues, yellows and reds of their chequered and braided costumes stand out vibrantly from the crowd. Faces, half concealed behind plain black masks, are topped with straw hats, brims pinned back with plumed favours.

The harlequin figures we make to 'people' various key positions at the ball are not difficult to assemble with the aid of a photocopier. The cover of a magazine and a booklet about Venice supplied us with our images. They are gradually scaled up on the photocopier until we have about two dozen sheets of the disparate parts of each figure to place together like a jigsaw until each figure is whole. Keeping the shapes of the figures lined up fluently, these sheets are then glued together with wallpaper paste.

Next, the paper figures are cut out around their outer edges and laid out flat on to sheets of hardboard cut to the height and breadth of each figure. After drawing around each outline, they are lifted away and the drawn edge is meticulously cut through with a jigsaw. The figures are then pasted on to these wooden shapes and coloured in with crayons. A good coating (which should include the cut edges) of a syrupy varnish completes them, giving a yellowing, antiqued look.

TOPIARY TREES
IN ORDER TO FORMALIZE THE VAST QUANTITIES OF GREENERY I WANTED TO INTRODUCE, WE HAVE BUILT UP GREAT CONES OF TOPIARY TREES TO LINE UP ALONG THE LENGTH OF THE TABLE. COARSE CHICKEN WIRE IS CUT INTO LARGE, TALL TRIANGLES WHICH ARE BENT AROUND SO THAT THE ROUGH WIRE EDGES LOCK INTO ONE ANOTHER TO FORM CONE SHAPES. SMALL BRANCHES OF LEAVES ARE THEN POKED IN TO COVER THE WHOLE OF ITS SURFACE. PUSHED SLIGHTLY TOGETHER, THE BASES OF THESE 'TREES' SIT FIRMLY IN SHALLOW WOODEN OVAL VESSELS. SOARING ABOVE THE TABLE, THEY MARK OUT ITS GREAT LENGTH.

THE DECORATIONS

It was the custom long before the advent of Prince Albert's German Christmas tree for the window of every house in Cornwall to display a kissing bough. To see this simple, but quite fetching device of two rings of greenery, interlocked at right angles, suspended at a window was commonplace. Clad in evergreens, firs and winter blossoms and hung with fruit, a candle was set within it where the two rings crossed.

I use this principle to construct the huge spheres to hang over the table and I cover them with the same greenery as the conical trees. The aim is to follow the medieval practice of decking out the halls like a woodland grove, while also giving the grand, artificial formality of topiary. Another sphere hangs in the entrance enclosing mistletoe, a true kissing bower.

The ceremonial yule log still burns in the great fireplace; it is supposed to burn continuously until Twelfth Night. It would be marked out

The long table is dressed in its gold-and-scarlet cloth and decked out in greenery in the form of pyramids and spheres, flanking a massive bowl of acid green hellebores. Green dishes hold nuts with gilded shells, and gilded fircones are studded with minute cushions of bright silks (far left). This mask is formed from stencilled eau-de-nil silk. It has an extended frill of gold mesh, and fanned out behind the spread-eagled wings of a bird are sprays of fragile dried flowers in a sharp yellow (above).

The bay tree is constructed over a Japanese wired paper globe lightshade fixed to a narrow, lichen-covered log. This is nailed through the solid bottom of the basket which is trimmed with small golden cones. Large magnolia leaves have been sprayed with bronze metallic paint to age them and stuck on to the paper shade to cover it completely (middle).

A huge dish of 'blazing raisins' flamed with brandy presents the challenge to grab them while they are on fire - a childhood dare (below).

early in the year and kept, to be carried aloft into the house at Christmas with great aplomb. Against a backdrop of greenery, 'The Holly and the Ivy' will ring out in this imposing room, accompanied by a small wind ensemble.

Greeted with the proverbial steaming bowl of punch, the guests then enjoy venison with root vegetables, fruits and nuts and special Christmas sweetmeats. Before the 'carriages' at dawn they will be offered breakfast, fine moulds of saffroned kedgeree garnished with prawns and parsley.

THE TALL WAXY YELLOW CANDLES WHICH LIGHT THE LONG DINING TABLE ARE EMBELLISHED WITH THE ETERNAL VINE. ITS CLASSIC FORM ENTWINES THESE IVORY COLUMNS WITH GRAPES, LEAVES AND TENDRILS MARKED IN GOLD PAINT. A STENCIL OF OUR GRAPE BORDER IS GLUED AND WRAPPED AROUND EACH CANDLE IN TURN, EDGES FASTENED WITH MASKING TAPE. WITH VERY GENTLE SPRAYING, A DENSE LAYER OF GOLD PAINT IS GENTLY BUILT UP TO DEFINE THE PATTERN THROUGH THE CUT SHAPES. WHEN THE PAINT IS DRY, THE STENCIL IS CAREFULLY REMOVED TO REVEAL THE SHEER BEAUTY OF THE GOLD FIGURED ACROSS THE SMOOTH PALE WAXY SURFACE. WHEN THE CANDLE IS ALIGHT, THE WAX GLOWS WARMLY NEAR THE FLAME, THROWING UP THE GOLDEN PATTERN CLEARLY. THESE BURNISHED CANDLESTICKS LIGHT UP THE FULL LENGTH OF THE GREAT OAK TABLE.

A tiny dance card, decorated with pieces of gold-embossed paper cut from doilies, has a slim gold pencil attached to it by a cord. Marking each dance down to a particular partner, it revives a decorous, old-fashioned practice (right).

As well as the row of tall candles on the table, there are dotted about among the dishes some on a different scale. Mottled in deep greens and ambers, these wax shapes take the form of cubes and squared towers. They have a particularly rich texture as they have been treated to a coat of lace stencilling. This is done by using a piece of lace as a resist to spray paint, a method that imparts a delicate but concise design over each surface.

In keeping with the evening's theme of borrowed grandeur, we use appealing souvenirs from Florence – candlesticks and small trays are particularly apt. Painted with false antiquity in dirtied mellow creams, dull pinks and aquamarines, they are chequered with gold over embossed wood.

Now the scene is a setting for revelry, not perhaps the measured steps of a sedate minuet that no doubt was once performed within these walls, nor even, I hope, the pallid valeta or the raucous, snaking conga, but rather the exuberant Scottish reels that whirl away the hours. When midnight strikes in a lower hall, hands are grasped and circles formed as 'Auld Lang Syne' is sung. The voices sing for the proverbial 'cup of kindness', an expression of true hospitality.

For the arrival of first footers, the first people of the New Year to set foot over the threshold, I propose a visit from some Masqueraders, a troupe of players with an ancient performance that predates Christianity. Drawn into the great hall, a circle is formed about the fire as the players set to, unravelling their time-worn tale. Traditionally, as forerunners to our present-day pantomimes, the men dressed in period 'heirloom' dresses of their great-grandmothers and the girls turned out as sea captains and the like. For our performance, slashed, ruffled and puffed, brilliantly coloured coats and dresses are decked out with shining brass buttons and buckles, all this topped with cocked hats, gaily festooned with ribbons and streamers, plus colourful stockings and high-heeled boots. Our troupe of mummers take exotic parts and they play out the ritual of St George, vanquishing first the Turkish knight and then the dragon to win an Egyptian princess. An old play, symbolic of chasing off winter to allow for the miraculous revival of spring.

A *DRESSED CHAIR*
THIS HIGH-BACKED CHAIR HAS BEEN
SPECIALLY DRESSED-UP FOR THE
PARTY, ITS ENVELOPING COAT OF
FELT REACHING TO THE FLOOR.
QUITE ORDINARY REPRODUCTION
STRAIGHT-BACKED DINING CHAIRS
WITH LEATHERETTE SEATS AND
GRAVY-BROWN VARNISH CAN BE
TRANSFORMED, CINDERELLA-STYLE,
WITH THIS FLAMBOYANT COVER-UP.
THE CHAIR'S BASIC MEASUREMENTS
ARE CAREFULLY NOTED AND
TRANSLATED INTO A PAPER PATTERN
IN THE SHAPE OF A CROSS WITH
FLARED-OUT ENDS. FROM A GOOD
SWATCH OF FELTS I SELECT MY
FAVOURITE EAU-DE-NIL COLOUR;
MARRIED WITH SOME SUBTLE
PATTERNING OF GOLD DECORATION,
IT HAS A CLASSIC ITALIAN LOOK.
SPRAYED BORDERS ARE MARKED OUT
ON THE FELT IN SOLID BANDS OF
GOLD, INITIALLY DOUBLE THE WIDTH
BUT THEN FOLDED IN HALF AND
STUCK DOWN WITH FABRIC ADHESIVE
TO GIVE THE EDGES SUBSTANCE. THE
TREE OF LIFE, THE SAME STENCIL
DESIGN AS USED FOR THE COVER OF
THE GREAT TABLE, IS THEN APPLIED
ACROSS THE REMAINING SURFACE
AND OVERPRINTED WITH A DENSER
DESIGN OF LACE. PLACED OVER THE
CHAIR, THE COVER IS TIED INTO
PLACE WITH A BROAD, RAVISHINGLY
GILDED COTTON SASH.

STENCILLED FELT CLOTH
THE FLAMBOYANT PATTERNED
CLOTH WHICH IS THROWN OVER THE
WHOLE LENGTH OF THE SUPPER
TABLE MAKES AN EXTRAVAGANT
IMPRESSION. THIS IS QUITE AT
VARIANCE WITH THE ORDINARINESS
OF THE MATERIALS USED IN ITS
MAKE-UP. A BALE OF FELT IS
STENCILLED ALL OVER WITH GOLD
SPRAY PAINT. THIS LARGE-SCALE
DESIGN, BASED ON THE CLASSIC
JACOBEAN TREE OF LIFE, WAS
ORIGINALLY CREATED FOR THE
WALLS OF OUR DINING ROOM. HERE,
ON FELT, IT IMMEDIATELY IMPARTS A
GRANDEUR NOT GENERALLY
ASSOCIATED WITH SUCH A HUMBLE
MATERIAL, TAKING IT INTO A
CATEGORY OF SUMPTUOUS
BROCADES AND CUT VELVETS. THE
FLOWING FORMS MARKED OUT IN
GOLD GLEAM IN THE SOFT LIGHT OF
THE CANDLES, EXPRESSING ONCE
MORE THE ETERNAL APPEAL OF THIS
AGELESS METALLIC FINISH.

INDEX

Abbey Hotel 23
Alsia 46, 47
angels 135, 139, 143
anniversary presents 128
apples 63, 73, 111, 113, 118, 119, 127, *see* dried apple rings
arches 47, 56
Aunt Sally 81, 92
autumn 7, 110-33

backdrop
    Indian 88, 91
    stencilled tenting 56-9
barn raising 131
baskets 25, 41, 92, 117, 127, 133, 144, 145
Bath Oliver biscuits 127
beachcomber's throne 101
beach paraphernalia 107-9
beach party 100-9
beach towel 109
Boscean 47
Botticelli 28, 97, 98
boxes, decorative 23, 87, 138
buckets, decorated 23, 83
bunting 93

cake boxes 87
cake stall 81, 84-7
cake stand 85
candelabra 144
candles 9, 11, 118, 119, 131, 140, 143, 154, 157
candlesticks 144, 154
card, Valentine 19, 21, 22
carnival 94-9
    float 94, 97, 98-9
    history 97
carol singing 134, 139
Carter, Harry 67-8
chairs, decorated 25, 33, 155
chicks' pavilion 28, 29

children's decorations 142-3
china, painted 90, 91
china paints 90
chocolate box, decorated 23
christening 10-17
    cake 16
    presents 11, 13, 14, 15
    robe 14
    tea 16
Christmas 134-45
    angels 135, 139, 143
    candles 140, 143
    carol singing 134, 139
    crackers 141
    decorations 137, 142-3, 144
    decorative boxes 138
    food 137, 144
    presents 140
    pudding 137, 144, 145
    toys 142, 143
    traditions 143
    yule log 152-3
collage sheets 8, 13, 21, 27, 39, 53, 65, 77, 81, 97, 103, 113, 123, 137, 149
colours, combining 8
corn dolly 113, 114, 115, 119
cornucopia 119
corrugated cardboard 133
costumes
    Masked Ball 149, 154
    pirate 63, 65, 68-9
crackers 141
curtains 17, 133
    tie backs 17
cushions 9, 37
    fan-shaped coral 104, 108
    border 40-1
    minute 153
    round with piping and apple blossom 40-1
    sea design 77

daisy chain 43
dance card 154
decorated buckets 23, 83
decorated chairs 25, 33, 155
decorative boxes 23, 87, 138
découpage 30, 129
doily 22, 23, 27, 35, 85, 86, 87, 139, 154
dried apple rings 84, 87

Easter 24-35
    bonnets 25, 27, 29, 34, 35
    eggs, decorated 24, 25, 30, 31

feathers 9, 150
fireplace 126, 143
firescreen 128-9
first footers 154
float *see* carnival
Florence 97, 154
flowerpots 56, 79, 82, 83, 90, 91
font 14
Frenchman's Creek 68
Furry Dance, The 49

games 43, 70-1
garden fête 78-93
    Aunt Sally 81, 92
    cake stall 81, 84-7
    garden stall 78, 79, 81, 82-3
    White Elephant stall 81, 88-9
garden sieve, stencilled 82
garden tubs 78, 82-3
garlands 46, 49, 51, 126
gingerbread 85, 86, 87, 142, 143
gingham 37, 40, 41
Godolphin 149, 150-1
golden wedding 120-9
    firescreen 128-9
    presents 128

gold paint 9, 16, 17, 23, 124, 139, 140, 143, 144, 154, 155, 157
guess the name of the doll 79, 88
guess the weight of the cake 86

hammock 104, 109
harlequins 150, 151
harvesting 114-17
Harvest Supper 110-19
    breads 114, 115
hats
    crêpe paper 141
    pirate 73
Helston 49
Holy Wells 14, 45; *see also* well dressing; Alsia
hops 126
housewarming 131-3
how many sweets in a jar 79, 88

interfacing 13, 15, 61
Italian Renaissance 97

Jamaica Inn 68
jam pot covers 85
Jolly Roger 70, 73

kissing bough 137, 152
kites 62, 65, 101, 107

lace 9, 19, 22, 23, 139, 150, 154, 155
Lamorna valley 144
lamps 133
lampshade 124, 153
lanterns 116-17, 150
    paper 142-3
lavender bags 128, 129
Lenten fasting 95

make-up, pirate 69
Marizion 68

masks 146, 147, 150, 153
Masqueraders 154
materials, choosing 8
May Day 36-43, 45, 49
    bringing home the May 49
    maypoles 39-43
    May Queen 37, 43
    picnics 41-3
Minack theatre 7, 75, 76
mirror frame 127
Mothering Sunday 29
Mousehole 97

name panel 14
napkins 9, 61
    rings 114
neck of corn 115
Newlyn artists 43, 55, 61
New Year's Eve 146-57
    costumes 149, 154
    dance card 154
    decorations 152-3
    first footers 154
    harlequins 150, 151
    masks 146, 147, 150
    Masqueraders 154
nosegays 126
nuts, golden 140, 141, 144, 153

oranges 126, 135, 140, 144
    wooden 145

Padstow 39
palm trees, artificial 104, 105
paper chains 142
parrot 65, 72, 73
party games 43, 70-1
Penzance 23, 92, 127, 134, 151
    Silver Band 92, 134
picnic baskets 41, 109
picnic trays 8, 76-7
pincushion 14
pirate party 62-73
    costumes 63, 65, 68-9
    food 73

games 70-1
hats 73
Jolly Roger 70, 73
kite 62, 65
make-up 69
parrot 65, 72, 73
props 65, 73
raft 66, 67, 70
skull-and-cross-bones 62, 71, 73
tales 67-8
treasure chest 65, 70, 71
treasure map 65, 70, 71
Pirates of Penzance 65
plant trays 78, 79, 82
pomanders 126, 140
Porthcurno 47
presents
    christening 11, 13, 14, 15
    Christmas 140
    golden wedding 128
    housewarming 131, 132, 133
pre-theatre picnic 74-7
Prussia Cove 67
Punch-and-Judy show 81

Queen of May 37, 43

rabbit hutch 32, 33
raft 66, 67, 70
ribbons 8, 9, 13, 15, 21, 22, 27, 35,
    36, 37, 49, 50, 70, 87, 128,
    138, 139, 140, 143, 150
rick building 115-17
ricrac braid 15, 23, 53
rug, stencilled 77

St Audrey 46
St Buryan/Beriana 46, 47
St George 154
St Michael's Mount 23
St Patrick 46
St Piran 46
St Valentine's Day 19-24
    cards 22
    history 23

presents 21, 22, 23
sampler 13
Sancreed 14, 55
sarongs 106-7
scarves 63, 68-9
Scillonion 7
screen 124
shells 98, 103
    as stencils 98, 99
    on treasure chest 71
Shrove Tuesday 95
simnel cake 29
smuggling 67-8
spring 7, 10-49
stencilling 9
    bucket 23
    cake boxes 87
    candles 140, 154
    canvas 98, 99, 107
    chair cover 155
    counterpane 28
    curtain tie backs 17
    cushions 77, 104, 108
    garden sieve 82
    hats 73
    jam pot covers 85
    napkins 61
    palm trees 104, 105
    picnic trays 76
    pudding bowl covers 86
    ribbons 15, 35, 138
    rug 77
    sacking 71, 117
    sarongs 106-7
    screen 124
    silk mask 153
    tablecloths 16-17, 40, 121, 124,
    157
    tenting backdrop 56-9
    towel 109
    umbrella 77
    watering can 82
    wrapping paper 129, 139, 140
storage jars as lamps 133
summer 7, 50-109

tablecloths 9
    checked, with blossom 37, 40
    coral patterned 104
    flower stencilled 28
    gold 16-17
    gold and scarlet 153, 156-7
    hessian 117
    quilt-like 61
    vine 120, 121, 124
    tee-shirts, stripy 63, 68, 69
    terracotta flowerpots 56, 79, 82,
    83, 90, 91, 143, 144
Thomas Hardy 117
topiary trees 152
towel, beach 109
toys 142, 143
treasure chest 65, 70, 71, 150
Treasure Island 65, 68
treasure map 65, 70, 71
Twelfth Night 143, 145, 152

umbrella, stencilled 77
urns 123

vine 120, 121, 123, 124, 125,
    154
Venice 151
Venus 98, 98
violets, crystallized 19

waste-paper bin 129
watering can 78, 82
wedding 50-61
    cake 60, 61
    see also golden wedding
well dressing 44-9; see also Holy
    Wells, Alsia
wheat-stack pudding 119
White Elephant stall 81, 88-9, 91
wind-shelter 107-9
winter 7, 134-57
wrapping paper 15, 28, 128, 129,
    133, 138, 139, 140, 142

yule log 152-3

ACKNOWLEDGMENTS

My grateful thanks to:

Chris Baker who arrived smiling from Paris bearing specialities like sugared almonds.

IN PENZANCE
Clare Harford who worked closely with me, adding her extravagant imagination so freely.
The spirited team of regulars and irregulars, Raymond, Bec, Karen, Helen, Katie, Matt, Peter, Joanna, Stephanie and Emmy.
Julie Whitt for her continuously thoughtful planning, and the typing feat.
The turn-out of beautiful children and the generous loan of beautiful places:
Godolphin, Tereife, Boskenna, The Minack and the fisherman's hut at Cape Cornwall.
The Penzance Silver Band and Claude Nicholas.
Anthea Wright, Horas Kennedy, Margaret Price, Geraldine Jones, Hilaria Honess.
Daphne's Antiques, Harris's Bistro, Richmonds Restaurant, Manzis Jewellers, Mounts Bay Wine Company.

IN COVENT GARDEN
Anne Furniss and Mary Evans whom I so much enjoyed working with, and to Sue Storey for her painstaking work on the book design; also to Louise Simpson and Patsy North for their meticulous input.

SUPPLIERS
The Stencilled House
Offray Ribbons

Lyn Le Grice Stencil Design - stencil supplier, courses and interior design.